THE JEWISH PEOPLE

HISTORY · RELIGION · LITERATURE

THE JEWISH PEOPLE
HISTORY • RELIGION • LITERATURE

Advisory Editor
Jacob B. Agus

Editorial Board
Louis Jacob
Jacob Petuchowski
Seymour Siegel

JESUS
AS OTHERS SAW HIM

BY
JOSEPH JACOBS

ARNO PRESS
A New York Times Company
NEW YORK • 1973

Reprint Edition 1973 by Arno Press Inc.

Reprinted from a copy in
  The Princeton Theological Seminary Library

THE JEWISH PEOPLE: History, Religion, Literature
ISBN for complete set: 0-405-05250-2
See last pages of this volume for titles.

Manufactured in the United States of America

———◆———

Library of Congress Cataloging in Publication Data

Jacobs, Joseph, 1854-1916.
    Jesus as others saw Him.

    (The Jewish people: history, religion, literature)
    Published in 1903 under title: As others saw Him.
    Reprint of the ed. published by B. G. Richards,
New York.
    1. Jesus Christ--Fiction. I. Title. II. Series.
PZ3.J1544Je5 [PR6019.A334]   813'.4   73-2211
ISBN 0-405-05275-8

JESUS
AS OTHERS SAW HIM

A RETROSPECT A.D. 54

"It cannot be that a prophet
perish out of Jerusalem."
—Luke xiii. 33

BY

JOSEPH JACOBS

PREFACE BY ISRAEL ABRAHAMS
Cambridge University

INTRODUCTORY ESSAY BY
HARRY A. WOLFSON
Harvard University

NEW YORK
BERNARD G. RICHARDS CO., Inc.
1925

PREFACE

PREFACE TO THE NEW EDITION

The author of this fascinating fantasy, now re-printed, was wont to make a claim, high indeed, but as just as it was high. "The spiritual walls of the English Ghetto," wrote Joseph Jacobs in 1896, "have only fallen during the present generation. I may lay claim, I think, to have been almost the first who stepped outside, and regarded the position of Judaism from the standpoint of Modern Thought. Others have followed, and there is every sign of a rise of a New Judaism which attempts to combine fidelity to Jewish History with the requirements of Modern Thought and Culture."

He was equipped for this pioneer adventure both by his qualities and by their defects. He was "Senior Moralist" in Cambridge in 1876, and yet his first post was the secretaryship of the Society of Hebrew Literature. He was a pupil on the one hand of Henry Sidgwick and of John Ward, and on the other of Steinschneider and of Moritz Lazarus. His many-sidedness was so conspicuous that when Israel Zangwill in 1916 spoke his noble Memorial Address, he with equal seriousness and whimsicality said among many other brilliant things that future investigators —observing the variety and extent of his publications—will be tempted to disbelieve in a single Joseph Jacobs, but credit his works to many Joseph Jacobs's. There is only one questionable epithet in the whole

of Mr. Zangwill's Address—he characterizes Jacobs
as "profound." Jacobs's lack of profundity was as
obvious as his possession of wide tastes and in-
terests. Nay, the defect grew out of the quality. He
saw, and saw swiftly, too vast a field to be a patient
observer of details. At all events, one type of pioneer
gains in efficiency when he is a surveyor in the big
sense rather than in the small sense. Jacobs himself
quoted with approval the epigram: "It is only the
superficial who do not judge by what lies on the
surface." No scholar has been more inaccurate than
he; no man of letters more sure and sound and true
in his perceptions and generalizations. As with
Geiger, his conclusions will survive, though the
premises on which his results were based already
need revision.

It is his quality of perception rather than the defect of indifference to detail that shines forth in his
one imaginative composition, "Jesus As Others Saw
Him." The detail is here, as well as the perception.
Why did he write the book? Mention has been made
of Mr. Zangwill, and the clue is supplied by that
name. In 1893 came the "Children of the Ghetto,"
and Zangwill's fame was established. Jacobs was
challenged by his friends. "You are always writing
about romances, but can you write a romance of your
own?" He accepted the challenge. But he would
not choose as subject the modern Ghetto life. He
preferred to turn to the ancient environment in which
moved and taught the Jew who has influenced the
great world more than any other of his race. We
need not seek to evaluate Jesus in order to concede
so much as that. But there is a difficulty. Though
Jesus affectionately thought of himself as offering

the evangel of the Kingdom to "the lost sheep of the house of Israel," the World requited Israel's rejection of its own child by a long drawn out animosity. Israel refused the rôle of lost sheep, and so was found and sent to the slaughter by the World. Both Israel and the World came to forget that Jesus was a Jew, that his doctrine for the most part displayed, in Jacobs's own terms, an "essential Jewishness." Because Jews refused the Pauline Christ they ignored the Jesus of the Synoptics; because the World adored the Christ it, too, belittled his Jewishness. Jacobs realized the need of changing both sides of this negation; of inducing the brethren of Jesus to reclaim him, and the followers of Jesus to replace him in his Jewish environment.

The charm of Jacobs's presentation derives from his admiration of Jesus on the one hand and, on the other hand, his appreciation of what Jesus owed to his Jewish ancestors and contemporaries. He used all available materials, the Logia and the Gospels, the Hebrew Bible and the Rabbinic traditions. It is wonderful how much Jacobs had read. If he is wrong in detail, he is brilliantly wrong. It is scarcely credible that Jesus antagonized the people finally against him by declining to countenance the withholding of tribute money from Rome. Jesus thus withdrew from the rôle of Liberator; the people who would have followed him stepped back in despair. "During Holy Week," writes Jacobs, "Jesus successively alienated every section of the Jewish nation. On Monday he attacked the power of the priests, on Tuesday that of the Pharisees, while on Wednesday he set the common people against him by refusing to countenance their hopes of freedom from the Romans by acquiescing in the payment of tribute to them." In this summary, we miss the alienation of Rome. Was this not because of the Messianic claim, with its political undercurrent of revolt against Roman rule? Yet, in quite another way, the silence of Jesus as to his Messianic character is treated by Jacobs as contributory to his death. Israel in the ages to come would know Jesus as his greatest son. "And in that day he will say unto thee, O Jesus: My sons have slain thee, O my son, and thou hast shared our guilt." Apparently, Jacobs reasons (in the mouth of course of the narrator, not of the author) that if Jesus had spoken out, Israel would perhaps have accepted him. Israel expected and required a conquering Messiah, Jesus thought of the suffering Servant. Why did Jesus refrain from expounding his ideas? "The death of Jesus was a sublime suicide." In other words, Jesus' assumption of the Messianic rôle first attracted the people and then his refusal of the rôle alienated them. He was silent because he conceived the rôle in terms other than theirs. And his silence led to Calvary. How much significance Jacobs assigned to the tribute money is illustrated by his choice of the coin to adorn the front cover of the first edition.

It is all more ingenious than convincing. But it makes delightful reading, and a wide circle of Jews and Christians will assuredly enjoy this presentation of a masterpiece in a new issue. Only one comment more will be made here. The first edition of the book was published anonymously. The omission of the author's name from the title-page was not due to timidity. He regarded the book as a *ballon d'essai,* and it failed at the time to attract the lightning.

Later on, he frankly acknowledged the provenance of the volume; he thought it his best composition, as indeed it is. But the real Jewish entry into the exposition of the Synoptic Gospels had to wait for fourteen years after Jacobs published his daring portraiture of the heroic figure which gives the Gospels their eternal vogue. In 1909 Mr. Claude G. Montefiore published his two epoch-making volumes on the Synoptic Gospels. This was the first appearance in the world of scholarship of a Jewish Commentary on Mark, Matthew and Luke. It was Montefiore, not Jacobs, who won a hearing for Jews regarding the great Oriental whom the West reveres. Montefiore, unlike Jacobs, unlike the rest of us of his generation, did not step outside the Ghetto, for he never was in it. He, and not another, was the destined spokesman of Jewry as to the Jewish side of the heart and mind of Jesus. The right of entry has been won; Jews are becoming reconciled to Jewish presentations of Jesus, Christians so far from resenting, welcome them.

But though another and not Joseph Jacobs opened this door, the latter saw at least that the door ought to be opened. He approached the adventure well armed, less with weapons of offence and defence, than with the disarming forces of sympathy and understanding. To open doors, the open mind is the master-key. Not by warfare but by common love will the secret of Jesus and of his place in history and in life be laid bare. Jacobs was no weakling in faith, he was a stalwart son of the Synagogue. But he invisaged the Synagogue as an expanding edifice, in one of whose many mansions there was a place of honour for him who was rejected of men, and whose brothers men have rejected because of him. Across the ages Joseph Jacobs stretched a comrade's hand—an impotent gesture, perhaps, but a gesture inspired by the lovable and tolerant spirit of the modern Jewish scholar who made it.

I. ABRAHAMS.

INTRODUCTORY

HOW THE JEWS WILL RECLAIM JESUS

Throughout the history of religious controversies between Christians and Jews in the Middle Ages Christianity was on the defensive. The Christians considered themselves called upon to prove the claims they made on behalf of Jesus by endeavouring to show that the vague prophetic promises were all fulfilled in Christ. The Jews had no counter claims to make; they simply refused to be impressed. As the historical custodians of the Bible text as well as of its manifold interpretations, the Jews looked rather amazed and at times even amused at the confidence with which the erstwhile heathen interpreted at their own pleasure the mistaken Scriptures quoted from the Vulgate. This attitude of aloofness and incredulity was sufficient to enrage even saints among Christians, for it gave them an uneasiness of feeling, deepening into fear and doubt and a general sense of discomfort, which explains much of the Christian intolerance of the Jews. The great victories achieved by Christianity, its conquest of many youthful barbarian races and its destruction of many effete civilizations—all this did not compensate its adherents for their failure to win over the handful of survivors of the race that had witnessed the birth of Christianity. And so the Jews were dragged to churches and to royal courts to listen to sermons and to partake in disputations in order to be impressed and become convinced.

Today we Jews have taken the burden of proof upon ourselves. A century of infiltration of Christian ideas into our life through all the agencies of education has robbed us of our essential Jewish character, of our distinctively Jewish philosophy of life, and has left us Jews only in appearance, in occupation and in the semblance of an external social coherence. In everything that guides our life and determines our view thereof, we have become thoroughly Christianized, for we have all accepted Christ if not in the theological sense of a savior at least in the historical sense of a civilizer. We have all fallen in with the prevalent view that Christianity is essential to the progress of human civilization, which is, after all, another version of the orthodox belief that Christ is necessary for the salvation of our soul. If indeed we do not openly acknowledge that Christ has fulfilled the promises of the prophets, we proceed on the assumption that modern civilization is the fulfillment of the promises of Christ. And everything we imagine nowadays that we see in the utterances of Christ we assume to have been contained in them from the beginning and to have been obvious to everyone who stood by and listened. We thus wonder at the blindness of our forefathers, the eye witnesses of Christ, for not seeing all this. We ask ourselves, why did they not accept Jesus?

From this question it is only another step to the greater question, why should we not accept Jesus? There are many among us who, while not quite convinced that civilization has already fulfilled the promises of Christ—for occasionally facts stare us

in the face and awaken us from the spell of words—
still believe in the potency of Christ's sayings, a
potency almost magical, by which the world is yet
to be saved. We seem to think with the rest of the
sentimental part of Christendom that evil can be
cured not by removing its causes but by exhortation
and by calling to repentance and to a closer study
of the sayings of Jesus. If we are sometimes re-
minded that as Jews we are already supplied with a
complete assortment of similar sayings by the rabbis,
Mr. Claude Montefiore answers for us, in effect, that
it is easier for the modern Jew to learn Hellenistic
Greek than rabbinic Hebrew.

We thus have two questions: Why did not the
Jews accept Jesus? Why should not the Jews accept
Jesus?

Of the historical question there are many attempted
solutions. All these solutions, however, proceed upon
the hypothesis that there were certain elements in
the teachings of Jesus which made them *a priori*
unacceptable, if not repugnant, to the Jews of his
time. It is sometimes said that it was due to the
fact that Jesus was too willing to render unto
Cæsar the things which were Cæsar's, as if the Jews
of that time, and immediately after, were at one in
their open defiance of the powers that be. More
often it is said that the boldness of his legal decisions
offended the sensibilities of the Law-abiding Jews,
as if the Law were already rigid and fixed by that
time and as if the Pharisees themselves were not torn
by internal dissensions which had almost divided the
Law into two Laws. Occasionally fine-spun specula-
tions are expended upon subtle distinctions between
the ethical teachings of Jesus and those of the lead-

ing contemporary Pharisees, distinctions in which one finds no greater difference than that between the negative form of the Golden Rule as given by Hillel and its positive form as given by Jesus. One would not like to become irreverent and dismiss the entire question by repeating with Pontius Pilate in Anatole France's *Le Procurateur de Judée:* "*Jésus, de Nazareth? Je ne me rappelle pas.*"

But what we should really like to know is what is exactly meant by the question of the Jewish acceptance of Jesus. The personality of Jesus as conceived in the manner of the various forms of christology could never find a place in Judaism, for it is altogether foreign to its fundamental principles and is a later importation from without. As the promised Messiah, if he ever claimed to be that, he simply did not meet the conditions which in the conception of the people of that time had to attend the coming of the promised Messiah. As a leading authority on questions of the Law, the contemporaries of Jesus could not be expected to accept Jesus more than they did Shammai or Hillel. As a moral and religious teacher, it seems that he succeeded quite well in attracting a goodly number of Jews of the lowlier station of life and culture among whom he appeared and to whom he delighted to deliver his messages. What really requires an explanation is not the paucity of Jewish followers but rather the great number of Gentiles that were soon to follow him or, rather, his idealized name.

The only intelligent meaning that a Jew may attach to the problem of the acceptance of Jesus is of a literary nature, namely, why were not the teachings of Jesus incorporated in Jewish literature together with those of other great teachers? One naturally would not expect them to be formed into a new book of the Bible, though he certainly did claim to be a prophet. Only those who are unacquainted with literary conditions in Palestine at that time and are accustomed to think of the New Testament as a continuation of the Old could ever dream of such a possibility. Jesus is not a rejected prophet, at best he is a rejected rabbi. Prophecy was supposed to have come to an end long before Jesus made his appearance. The Jews did not put a limitation to the books of the Bible in order to keep Jesus out; Jesus simply happened to come at a time when that body of literature in the opinion of the authorities of the time was practically closed. The question is merely, why were not the teachings of Jesus included in the Tannaitic collection of a subsequent generation which includes the teachings of men who lived at about the time of Jesus? To put it more concretely, why is the Sermon on the Mount not included in the collection of the *Sayings of the Fathers?* That Jesus had fallen from grace could not account for that omission, for Elisha ben Abuyah, too, fell from grace, and still he is quoted in that collection of traditional wisdom.

The answer seems to lie in the nature of the records which entered into the making up of the Tannaitic collection of ancient traditions.

The Tannaitic literary collections contain the teachings recorded in the name of individual authors from the time of Simeon the Just, a contemporary of Alexander the Great, to the early part of the third century after the Christian era. There is, however, a marked difference between the earlier

records and those of the period following the estab-
lishment of the school of Jabneh, after the fall of
Jerusalem. In the earlier period only those who
were officially at the head of the schools are quoted
by name, otherwise scholars are grouped together
and referred to as collective bodies. To this gen-
eralization there are only a few exceptions, for
which there is always an obvious explanation. In
the later period, individual scholars in great numbers,
whether official dignitaries in the schools or not, are
quoted by name. There is no doubt that in the
period from which the Tannaitic collections contain
only the common decisions of the schools transmitted
in the names of Bet Shammai and Bet Hillel (House
of Shammai, House of Hillel) but no teachings in
the name of individual scholars, there must have
been many individuals who in their private capacity,
unaffiliated with these two great schools, had taught
and preached in the synagogues, but whose teachings,
for lack of any agency for their collection and
preservation, were lost to the world. Jesus was one
of these unaffiliated teachers who taught and preached
during the period of the Bet Shammai and Bet
Hillel. If the teachings of Jesus were not similarly
consigned to oblivion, it is due to the fact that his
followers banded themselves, not into a sect, as it
is usually supposed, but into a "House," a Bet Jesus,
corresponding to the Bet Shammai and Bet Hillel,
and this "House" it was that collected and preserved
the teachings of Jesus just as the other "Houses"
collected and preserved the teachings of their re-
spective founders.

Once the teachings of Jesus were collected and
written down and were issued for public circulation,

which took place long before any official collection
of the Tannaim was allowed to be publicly circulated
in writing, they were declared by the leaders of the
Tannaitic schools as unauthorized writings, and were
put into the same class with all other unauthorized
works. It is thus not as an individual that Jesus was
excluded from the Tannaitic literary collections but
rather as an unaffiliated teacher, of no official position in any of the Tannaitic schools, who lived at
a time when, as a result of a general practice, the
teachings of that class of men were not included in
the official records of the schools which later made
up the Tannaitic collections.

By the same token the present day problem of the
Jewish acceptance of Jesus should be treated as a
problem of the reclamation of a lost literature rather
than that of the recognition of a new moral philosophy which is needful for our salvation. Good souls
always rush to gnomic sayings for guidance. Epic-
tetus and Marcus Aurelius, Confucius and the
Buddha, the rabbis and the folk sayings of every
nation are drawn upon for that purpose, though,
unlike the Sermon on the Mount, we are not expected
to make them into a creed. But gnomic sayings and
parables and homely examples hardly guide our lives.
All this kind of homespun wisdom was produced in
the infancy of mankind, in the simplicity of life, and
has been with us for centuries and in spite of it all
we have built up our atrocious civilization. If from
the complexity of our life we occasionally seek
refuge in the simple utterances with which the
sages of the past attempted to solve the difficulties
of their time, it is only painfully to realize how in-
adequate they are to solve the problems of today.

INTRODUCTORY

No economist, for instance, would take the view of Jesus on riches as a solution of the evils of accumulated wealth; or the examples of the fowls of the air and the lilies of the field as a remedy for unemployment; or the miracles of the feeding of the five and the four thousand as an alleviation of the blight of famine; nor would any medical man take the stories of the miraculous healings as a cure for all disease. A leader of liberal Christian thought has recently called upon Christians to give up the pretense that they seriously believe all the teachings of Jesus to be adequate as a practical guide of life.* Gnomic sayings, whether rabbinic or evangelical, are sufficient neither to change the human heart nor to alter conditions. At best they can be used only to adorn an economic report or to illustrate a sociological survey.

The Jewish reclamation of Jesus will not be brought about by efforts of evangelical piety on the part of some Jews, or by a sentimental yearning for what we haven't got, or by a servile imitation of the more powerful element in our environment. It will come about as a result of a wider and more comprehensive conception of the scope of Jewish learning and Jewish literature and of a general restoration of our lost literary treasures. When the works of Josephus, and the Apocrypha, and the Hellenistic writings have all been restored by us and given a place beside the hallowed literature of our tradition, then the works of Jesus also will find a place among them. It is not as a returning hero that Jesus will be restored, not as a beatified saint,—we shall not

* Kirsopp Lake: "Jesus" in *The Hibbert Journal* for October, 1924.

regret the past nor shall we apologize for our forefathers. But when with the revival of Jewish culture
and Jewish learning under free and unhampered conditions in a Jewish environment, painstaking Jewish
scholars, in an effort to reorganize and to reclassify
our literary treasures, will come to compile anthologies of the wise sayings and inspiring teaching
of our ancients, they will include among them the
sermons and parables of Jesus the Nazarene, the
Galilean rabbi who, like Philo and Josephus, has by
force of historical circumstances been for centuries
better known among non-Jews than among Jews.
The readers of those anthologies will pass on from
Talmudic and Midrashic selections to those of the
Gospels without being conscious of any difference,
except of such individual differences as mark the
sayings of men. The sayings of Jesus together
with the sayings of other rabbis will win their
way into the speech of the people, will become
blended and interwoven, and misquoted, after the
manner of such things,—for they all breathe the
same spirit. His sayings will be considered as part
of the maxims of the anonymous body of the wise,
of blessed memory, who express the national genius
of the people, not as those of an inspired individual
to be worshipped and exalted above all others.

And perhaps at that time our people will resume
their creative activity at the point it was nipped off,
in the time of the Mishnah and Midrash. If prophecy
will not return, the spirit of the Haggadah will again
rest upon our sages. Tired of the fettered forms of
verse and the diffuse forms of prose, we shall return
to our native original forms of expression. We
shall write text-books of science in the style of the

Mishnah, we shall compose works of erudition in the style of the Midrash, and we shall once more give expression to the great truths of life in the form of the Haggadah.

Then in a cloistered synagogue in a re-Judaized Galilee a sage, continuing the traditions of an ancient rabbi, will con over a new tome which will be an old tome revised. It will be a completed *Sayings of the Fathers,* recording the wisdom of the ages from the Men of the Great Synagogue to the men of the littlest of the synagogues, and among these will be included the sayings of the Alexandrian Philo and the Palestinian Jesus. He will read the utterances recorded in the name of Jesus the Galilean about the Pharisees and will say to himself: "O Rabbi Jesus, dost thou condemn the many for the sins of the few? Where is the quality of justice, not to speak of mercy?" But with characteristic Jewish charity he will quote from an ancient rabbi: "No man is taken to account for what he speaks in his distress." He will read his sayings about divorce and mutter: "O Rabbi Jesus, verily thou art a Shammaite; but we have long decided to follow the more lenient views of Hillel. We are not bound by thee." He will read his views about the Sabbath, and say: "Verily this is a precious sentiment of the rabbis, but where is the line to be drawn between the conflicting rights and the mutual obligations of institutions and individuals." And thus he will go on commenting in the spirit of an ancient rabbi. Then he will weave in a story in the fashion of a Haggadah: "Come and see, how great is the power of Israel. Once there was a child in Galilee. He was taken captive and carried off into the great city of Rome.

INTRODUCTORY

There they made a God of him; but some say they
made of him only a son of God, and others say only
a prophet of God. They built temples and churches
to his name in every land, and each nation worshipped
him according to its tongue, according to its manner and according to its custom. But the mind of
the child was not at rest until he returned to Galilee
and saw his name inscribed in an ancient tome among
the names of his castigated Pharisees. It is this
which Scripture says:"—and here an apt or an in-
apt quotation from the Scripture will follow.

This is how the Jews will reclaim Jesus.

HARRY AUSTRYN WOLFSON.

... the parables at which we have arrived must ... ... ended: the quest of the historical Jesus must go on.

FOREWORD

Owing to the behavior of many Christians, the name of Jesus is an anathema and a stumbling-block to the vast majority of Jews, even at the present day. The crimes committed against the Jews in the name of Christ have left their natural traces in the descendants of the victims of such inhumanity, the majority of whom indeed still suffer in one way or another from many who profess to follow Christ. It would scarcely be a matter to wonder at if the Jews absolutely abhorred the very name of Jesus. If they do not go so far as this, they yet ignore him almost entirely, and have a certain feeling of repulsion when called upon to consider his claims to be enrolled among their sages and saints. On the other hand, multitudes of Christians look upon Jews chiefly in the light of descendants of those "who killed Christ," and in the folk-mind there is left the impression that they would be willing to "kill Christ" again if the same succession of circumstances arose. By a natural transference of thought they are regarded as still engaged in "killing Christ"—that is, opposing the ideals represented by that specifically Jewish name, merely the Greek translation of Messiah.

Prejudice on the one side against prejudice on the other side has produced a veiled yet mutual antipathy which it would be as idle to ignore as it is desirable to eradicate. Recent events in France have shown to what length anti-Jewish prejudice on the part of Christians may lead men, but apart from the Dreyfus case there can be no doubt that these antipathies prevent in many cases that cooperation toward ideal justice at which the followers of both creeds profess to aim. To remove that prejudice from either side or from both is thus a pressing civic need.

It is the aim of the present study of part of the life of Jesus to assist toward this end by displaying to Jews the essential Jewishness of Jesus in many of his aspects, and by explaining to Christians how it came about that the leaders of the Jewish nation helped to put him to death. The writer would be the last person to imagine that a book of this kind could effect any radical change by itself, but such transformations of opinion come from reiteration from all sides, and the most persuasive part of the irenicon must always be that episode of Jewish history treated in the following pages.

The life of Jesus dealt with from the modern standpoint easily divides itself into three sections—the Legend, the Story, and the Myth. The first part deals with that kind of legendary exaggeration that clothes all heroes of tradition. The supernatural birth, the temptation in the wilderness, and the like, find their counterpart in numberless other quarters. The Myth, on the other hand—that view of the nature of Jesus which raises him to the demigods of antiquity, and reduces the mystical element of the mass or communion service to the blood covenant of savage or ancient clans—is also full of analogies with the creed or practise of other faiths. On these two points, the Legend and the Myth, there can be no hope of reconciliation between the Jewish and the Christian standpoint. What is known as the modern or critical view is ever approaching nearer the Jewish protest against the Christian claims in these regards.

But with regard to the Story of the life itself, there is no reason why substantial unanimity should not exist between Jews and Christians as to the historic reality of Jesus and as to the nature of his activity. On the one side it is idle to deny the substantial reality of the Gospel narratives. Facts require causes to explain them. As Matthew Arnold has shown, if we deny the authenticity of the Gospel sayings attributed to Jesus we only put the difficulty further back, and imagine an unknown ethical genius to have invented and attributed them to an imaginary or unimportant personage. On the other hand, it is difficult for Christians to understand how little novelty to Jews there is in the notes struck by Jesus—the Fatherhood of God, the spiritual excellence of poverty, and the like. Again and again his gnomes recall sayings of the contemporary rabbis, and the most recent discoveries have made it probable that the whole foundation of his ethical system was based on the Jewish "Two Ways" or catechism of his time, which is, therefore, given at full length in the following pages.

Another new source of knowledge of Jesus has been arrived at by researches in the outlying purlieus of theological learning and utilized in this book. Throughout the vast patristic literature are scattered a numerous set of sayings attributed to Jesus, and probably derived from lost Gospels or other sources having traditional connection with the Palestine of the first century. Many of these sayings have internal evidence in their favor, and all of them are of interest as showing the idea of the man held by the early church fathers. For this reason most of the more coherent sayings have been included in the two sermons inserted in this book. It may be curious, but it is not altogether inappropriate, that it should be left to a writer speaking from a Jewish standpoint to introduce to the ordinary English reader these new sources of knowledge about Jesus and his activity and opinions.

Yet, in a measure, this book is an anti-Gospel, and puts honestly, sincerely, and without reserve what can be said against what seem to the writer exaggerated claims put forward either for Jesus or by him. It is only by knowing exactly where we differ that we can hope ultimately to agree. But first and foremost the aim has been to arrive at some agreement as to the facts of the case. After these have been established we can commence to disagree as to their interpretation.

Joseph Jacobs.

To Aglaophonos, Physician of the Greeks at
Corinth, Meshullam ben Zadok, a Scribe of
the Jews at Alexandria, greeting : —

*It was a joy and a surprise to me to hear news
after many days from thee, my master and my
friend. To thee I owe whatever I have of Greek
wisdom ; for when in the old days at the Holy
City thou soughtest me for instruction in our
Law, I learnt more from thee than I could im-
part to thee. Since I last wrote to thee, I have
come to this great city, where many of my nation
dwell, and almost all the most learned of thy
tongue are congregated. Truly, it would please
me much, and mine only son and his wife, if thou
couldst come and take up thy sojourn among us
for a while.*

*Touching the man Saul of Tarsus, of whom
thou writest, I know but little. He is well in-
structed in our Law, both written and oral, having received the latter from the chief master
among those of the past generation, Gamaliel by
name. Yet he is not of the disciples of Aaron
that love peace ; for when I last heard of him he
was among the leaders of a riot in which a man
was slain. And now I think thereon, I am almost certain that the slain man was of the followers of Jesus the Nazarene, and this Saul was*

among the bitterest against them.   And yet thou writest that the same Saul has spoken of the Nazarene that he was a god like Apollo, that had come down on earth for a while to live his life among men.   Truly, men's minds are as the wind that bloweth hither and thither.

But as for that Jesus of Nazara, I can tell thee much, if not all.   For I was at Jerusalem all the time he passed for a leader of men up to his shameful death.   At first I admired him for his greatness of soul and goodness of life, but in the end I came to see that he was a danger to our nation, and, though unwillingly, I was of those who voted for his death in the Council of Twenty-Three.   Yet I cannot tell thee all I know in the compass of a letter, so I have written it at large for thee, and it will be delivered unto thee even with this letter.   And in my description of events I have been at pains to distinguish between what I saw myself and what I heard from others, following in this the example of Herodotus of Halicarnassus, who, if he spake rude Greek, wrote true history.   And so farewell.

CONTENTS.

I.

THE MAN WITH THE SCOURGE.

AS OTHERS SAW HIM.

I.

I was crossing one morning the Xystus
Bridge on my way to the Temple, when I
saw issuing from the nearest gate a herd
of beasts of sacrifice. Fearing that something untoward had occurred, I hurried to
the gate, and when I entered the Court
of the Gentiles, I found all in confusion.
The tables of the money-changers had
been overturned, and the men were gath-
ering their moneys from the ground. And
in the midst I saw one with a scourge in
his hand. His face was full of wrath and
scorn, his eyes blazed, and on his left temple stood out a vein all blue, throbbing
with his passion. He was neither short
nor tall, but of sturdy figure, and clad in
rustic garb.

Now, as the money-changers were es-
caping from his wrath, one of them ran

against a little child that was in the court,
and it fell screaming. The fellow took no
heed, but went on his course. But the
man with the scourge went to the little
child and raised it to its feet, and pressed
it to his side; the hand that rested on the
curly head was that of a workman, with
broken nails, and yet the fingers twitched
with the excitement of the man. But,
looking to his face, I saw that a wonderful
change had come over it. From rage, it
had turned to pity and love; the eyes that
had flashed scorn on the money-changers
now looked down with tenderness on the
little child. I remember thinking to
myself, " This man cannot say the thing
that is not; his face bewrayeth him."

Meanwhile the money-changers and
those with them had collected together
near the gate by which I had entered, and
stood there whispering and muttering
among themselves. All at once they
turned towards the man as he was sooth-
ing the little child, and shouted out together, "*Mamzer! Mamzer!*" which in
our tongue signifieth one born out of
wedlock. Then the man looked up from

the little child, his face once more full of
rage, and the blue vein throbbing on his
temple. He took a step towards the men,
and then he stopped. His face changed
to a look of pity, and the men themselves,
in fear and shame, slunk away before his
look through the gate and were gone.

Then he turned towards those that had
for sale doves as sacrifices for the women
and the poor. To these he spoke in a
tone that was calm and yet full of authority, and then I noticed that his voice
had the burr of our northern peasantry.
He said unto them, " Take these things
hence ; make not my Father's house a
house of merchandise." And these, too,
went away through the gates, carrying with
them the wicker cages full of doves. Ever
since that time the doves have been for
sale in Hanan's Bazaar on the Mount of
Olives.

Now I must tell thee that at this time
there had been much disputing between
the Pharisees and the Sadducees as to the
sale of beasts for sacrifice. The Pharisees
held that each man might buy such beasts
wherever he would; but the Sadducees,

being mainly priests, or of priestly blood,
would have it that the beasts of sacrifice
could only be purchased from the sales-
men duly authorized by the High Priest;
for they said, "Who shall tell that the
beasts are according to the Law, if they
are bought from any chance person?" Yet
many thought they only did this in order
that they might share the profit from the
sale of the animals. And, indeed, the
great riches of the High Priests came
mainly from this source. When, therefore, I saw the man with the scourge getting rid of these sacrificial animals from
the courts of the Temple, my first thought
was that he was of the sect of the Pharisees. Yet these are rarely found in the
country parts, and the man bore no great
marks of special piety; his phylacteries
were not broader than my own; the
fringes of his garment were not more conspicuous, nor did he seem as one of the
fanatics who are so many in our land. He
had done what he had done in all calm-
ness, and with a certain air of authority.
My wonder was aroused to think what
manner of man this could be, who did the

work of the Pharisees, and was not one himself.

While I thus thought, the man turned to a group of men clad in the same rustic garb, saying, " Be ye rather approved money-changers, holding fast the good and casting forth the false ; " [1] and, after other words, he turned from them and went up the steps leading to the Women's Court.

Now thou knowest, Aglaophonos, that at the entrance of this court standeth an inscription which saith, " LET NONE OF ALIEN BIRTH PASS WITHIN THE TEMPLE CLOISTERS : HE THAT TRANSGRESSES IS GUILTY OF DEATH." As the man with the scourge would enter the Women's Court, the Roman sentry stopped him, and pointed to this inscription with his spear. He shook his head, saying in faulty Greek, " Jewish I am," and showed the soldier the fringes of his garment after the Jewish fashion. Then the sentry drew back, and the man passed through.

Thereupon I went up to the men to

[1] This, like most other utterances of Jesus, found in this book but not in the Gospels, is also found in the early patristic literature. — ED.

whom the man with the scourge had
spoken, and greeted them with the greeting of peace.

"Peace unto thee, master," said one of
them in the same northern accent I had
noticed in their leader.

"Who is that man," I said, "that has
just gone into the Temple cloister?"

"Jesus of Nazara, in Galilee."

"And whose son is he?" I asked.

The man looked at his companions ere
he answered, —

"Of Joseph ben Eli the carpenter, and
Miriam his wife."

"And what is his trade?" I continued.

"A wheelwright," he said; "the best
wheels and yokes in all Capernaum are
made by him."

"But is he of the country-folk,[1] or a
pupil of the wise?"

"Nay, master, he knoweth the Law and
the Prophets."

"Of what party is he?   Boethusian he

---

[1] Ὄχλος τοῦ ἀγροῦ, seemingly the translation of the Hebrew עם הארץ used for those unlearned in the Law;
this term seems to have passed through much the same
history as "pagan." — ED.

cannot be, nor Sadducee; but is he Pharisee or Zealot, Essene or Baptist?"

" He is of no party."

" But from whom hath he received the
tradition of the elders? At whose feet has
he sat? Whom calleth he master?"

" He hath been baptized by Jochanan his
kinsman, but none calleth he master."

" If he have not the tradition, he cannot
teach the Law, for his words will not be
binding. Doth he sit in judgment or pronounce *Din?*"

" Nay, master, he but teacheth us to be
good."

" Ah," said I, "he is but a homolist
of the Hagada; he addeth naught to the
Halacha. Then what is his motto?"[1]

" He saith, ' Repent ye, for the kingdom
of heaven is at hand.'"

Then I took the man away from his companions, and out of hearing of the Roman
sentry, and asked him in a low tone, " And
who shall be the king thereof?"

But the man answered not, but said
only, " Lo! he cometh."

---

[1] Each of the Jewish rabbis used to sum up his teaching in some pregnant sentence. These are given in the
Talmudic treatise, *The Ethics of the Fathers.* — ED.

And, indeed, at that moment Jesus came
down by the steps he had ascended and
beckoned to his companions. And as they
went towards him I was surprised, and at
the same time horrified, to see amongst
them two persons whom I little thought to
find in any public place in Jerusalem, still
less in the courts of the Temple. One was
a woman in the yellow veil of a *hetæra;*
the other, a mere *Nathin* who had no
name among men, but was called *Dog o'
Dogs.* These two pressed close to Jesus;
the woman rushed forward with a sob and
raised the hem of his garment to her lips,
while to the man he spoke some friendly
words, smiling on him as they walked towards the entrance.

I was astonished. The man had seemed
so careful of the purity of the Temple that
he would not allow even the necessary
arrangements for its service to be performed in its precincts, yet he allowed its
courts to be defiled by the vilest of the
vile. Perchance, I thought, he had pre-
vailed upon them to perform the vows
enjoined by the Law, and cleanse themselves of their sin. Or was it that he was

ignorant of their characters, being but newly
come from rural parts? He must, indeed,
be different from other rabbis, who kept
themselves apart from all transgressors
against the Law till they had repented and
done penance.

While I thus meditated, I saw the High
Priest Hanan, whom ye Hellenes call Annas,
enter into the court of the Gentiles with his
guard. Thou rememberest the man, Aglaophonos — how his tyranny extended over
all the city. He was still called High Priest,
though Valerius Gratius, the Procurator,
had deposed him years before, lest haply he
might regain the regal power of the Maccabæans. Still, even after his deposition,
he had sufficient power to get his sons or
sons-in-law named High Priests. It was
one of the latter, Joseph Caiaphas, who at
that time held the office; yet the people
still called Hanan High Priest, and he himself wore on high days the bells and pomegranates round his tunic as a sign of his
dignity. Thou must remember his keen-
cut face, his nose like an eagle's, his long
white beard, bent neck, and sinewy hand.
Was it thou or I that first called him " the
Old Vulture"?

He had heard of the insult to his dignity
by the removal, without his orders, of the
money-changers and others to whom the
people paid the fees from which he and his
made such display in his grand dwelling
on the Mount of Olives. " Where is he?
where is he?" he cried, as he came bus-
tling up, with neck extended, and looking
more than ever like a bird of prey. He
soon found that the man he sought had
gone; but he had given his orders, and
before I left the court, I saw the money-
changers reënter and the cattle driven
back. I had to attend a meeting of the
Sanhedrim, for that year I had risen to the
third and highest bench of disciples who
sit under its members when they give judgment. Next year I was elected of the Seventy-One myself in the section of Israelites.
It must, therefore, have been in the six-
teenth year of Tiberius the Emperor,
nearly five-and-twenty years agone, that I
thus saw for the first time Jesus the Nazarene.

II.

THE UPBRINGING.

II.

THOU canst imagine the wonder and excitement in Jerusalem at this bold deed of the Nazarene. Not even the oracle of Delphi is regarded with so much reverence as our sacred fane, and none in our time had dared to interfere with its regulations, which have all the sacredness of our traditions. And of these none was regarded by the priestly guardians of the Temple as of greater weight for them than the right of sale of beasts of sacrifice. It is from this, as I have said, that the priestly order gain their wealth, and no more deadly blow could be struck at their power than to deprive them of this. Hence had the Pharisees protested against this right, but none had hitherto dared to carry out the protest in very deed. All the poor and all the pious would have been glad if they could buy their offerings to the Lord wheresoever they would.

But more than all, men of Jerusalem

were amazed at the daring of the Galilæan
stranger in opposing the High Priest Hanan. This man had been the tyrant of
the Temple and of the city for the whole
span of a generation of men, and no man
had dared say him nay for all that time.
Even the Romans, who had deposed him
from his position as High Priest, had not
dared to interfere with him otherwise. Yet
had this rude countryman, who had never
been seen, never been known to set foot in
Jerusalem before, dared to strike at the
root of his power and wealth. Thou canst
not wonder that men were curious to know
what manner of man he might be who
had dared this great thing, and busy
rumor ran through all the bazaars of
Jerusalem, asking, Who is this Jesus of
Nazara? All that I learnt of his kindred
and early life I learnt at this time, and I
here set it forth in order.

It was natural that I should first direct
my inquiries as to his birth, for the insult-
ing cry of the money-changers still rang
in my ears. Thou knowest our pride of
birth; I learnt from thee to abate it.
Every man in Israel taketh his place in

the nation according as he is a son of
Aaron or of Levi, a simple Israelite, or a
proselyte that fears the Lord; each man
knoweth his own and his neighbor's genealogy. The greatest slur upon a man is
to accuse him of "mixture," the greatest
insult is to call him "bastard." Why had
the money-changers cast this slur upon the
Nazarene? Thou and I, Aglaophonos,
who boast to be citizens of the Kosmos,
would not think the worse of him if the
taunt were true. Yet thou canst understand how great, even if he only thought
it to be true, would be the influence of
such a slur on this man's mind and on
his career. If in after-days he showed
himself so careless of the nation's hopes,
may it not have been that he felt himself
in some way outside the nation?

Now I found, upon inquiry among the
Galilæans settled in Jerusalem, that some
such scandal had arisen about his birth.
There had even been talk that Joseph ben
Eli would have put away his wife, but for
the stern penalties which our Law inflicts
upon the misdoer. Yet there may have
been naught but suspicion in the matter,

for the two lived together, and Miriam
bore several children to Joseph after this
Jesus.   But between him and them there
was never good will, and I have heard
things told of this Jesus which seem to
show some harshness in his treatment
of them, and even of his mother.   Once
when he was told that his mother and
brethren were without, and would see
him, he as it were repudiated them, saying,
" Who are my mother and my brothers?
Whosoever doeth the will of God, the
same is my brother and sister and mother."   Again, when once his mother
came to him and would speak to him, he
said to her, " Woman, what have I to do
with thee?"   The man whom I had seen
so tenderly thoughtful to a little child
could not have spoken thus unless he had
felt himself placed by some means outside
the natural ties of men.

Of Jesus' upbringing I could learn little.
When he was at the age of thirteen, when
each Jewish male child becomes a Son of
the Covenant (*Bar Mitzva*), and, as we
think, takes his sins upon his own soul, his
parents brought him to Jerusalem.   On

this occasion, as some still remember, he showed remarkable knowledge of the Law, when, as is customary, they read the portion of the Law set down for the Sabbath reading next after his birthday, and he was examined in its meaning by the learned men present. Yet he fulfilled not this promise of devotion to the Law as he grew in years. I cannot learn that he dusted himself with the "dust of the wise," as the sages have commanded.[1] Not having sat at the feet of any of the holders of tradition, he could not pronounce decisions of the Law.

His father brought him up to his own trade, that of carpenter. With us manual toil is not despised, as among you Hellenes; there is a saying among us, "Whoso bringeth not his son up to a handicraft traineth him for a robber." Jesus was a good and capable worker, and devoted himself especially to the making of yokes and wheels at Capernaum, where

---

[1] José ben Joeser said, "Let thy place be a place of meeting for the wise; dust thyself with the dust of their feet, and drink greedily of their teaching" (*Pirke Aboth*, i. 4). — ED.

he had settled, some five hours' journey
from his native place. Here he would
often read the *Haphtaroth,* or prophetical
lessons, in the synagogue, and explain it
after the manner of the Hagada.

Thus he would have passed his life, a
wheelwright on week-days, a preacher on
the Sabbath and festivals, but for a strange
event that occurred in his own family.
Among us Jews, none has more honor
than the *Nabi,* the man who speaks the
word of wisdom in the name of God.
How know we that a man is a Nabi?
Chiefly by his words, but mainly by his
eyes, in which there shines the light of
prophecy. Now, when Jesus was about
thirty years old, three or four years before
I first saw him, the light of prophecy came
in the eyes of his cousin, Jochanan ben
Zacharia Ha-Cohen. Thou knowest, Aglaophonos, that amongst us there is a sect
of Essenoi, who answer in much to the
Pythagoreans among the Hellenes. These
Essenoi eat no flesh, they dwell not in the
cities of men, they perform frequent lus-
trations, nor will they admit any into their
community until they have been baptized

of them ; they care little for the Temple
service, and in this above all distinguish
themselves from either Pharisees or Sadducees.   Their belief in the angels is
strong, and they use magic for the healing
of sickness.

Now, this Jochanan, the cousin of Jesus,
seems to have adopted in many things the
views of these Essenoi : he separated himself from men, and ate no flesh, nor did he
go up to the Temple on the three great
festivals of the year ; and above all, when
men began to follow after him, he would
admit none to communion with him till
he had baptized them in running water,
and for this he was called among the folk
Jochanan the Baptizer.   Yet he was not
an Essene, for he joined not their communion, nor established any distinction of
orders among the men who came out to
him ; he was more like unto the prophets
of old, who taught as individuals new
truths about life ; and his great teaching
was this : " Repent ye, for the kingdom of
heaven is at hand."   And men went out
to him, asking him in what they should
repent so as to become worthy of the

kingdom. Above all, those who were despised of the people because they did the
work of the Romans, by being their tax-
gatherers or their soldiers, feared the
wrath to come in the new kingdom which
he preached, and asked him in what they
should alter their ways. But to them he
was by no means hard, saying only to the
tax-gatherers, "Act justly," and to the
soldiers, "Do no violence." To the poor
he was tender and merciful, but exhorted
the rich to divide their possessions with
the poor. In this way he drew unto him
all who were despised of the people, and
those who were poor and miserable. Thus
he attracted the notice of the rulers, who
feared that he was preparing to rebel
against them ; for they said, "Wherefore
does this man attract to him the discon-
tented and the soldiery?"

Now, when the family of Jesus heard
that their relative was gaining a name
among men, they sent to Jesus, asking
him to go with them unto his cousin ; but
he, as I have heard, at first refused, saying,
"Wherein have I sinned, that I should be
baptized of Jochanan?" Yet afterwards

he consented unto this, and went out to
be baptized of his cousin. And when he
saw the power for good that Jochanan
exercised, his spirit was exalted, and he
felt that he too had within him the same
power. Many strange things have I heard
of what happened to this Jesus when he
submitted to be baptized by his cousin.
And as none but Jesus would have known
his feelings on that occasion, these reports
must have come from him. Among us it
is the custom that each Jew should select
from the Psalms some *stichos* which should
serve as the motto of his life, and identify
him when he appeareth before the Angel
of Death. Now, it would appear that as
Jesus was being baptized of Jochanan he
heard the Daughter [1] of the Voice of God
say to him the *stichos* of the psalm, "Thou
art my Son; this day have I begotten
thee." Whether this was a protest of his
soul against the slur cast upon his birth,
what man shall say? But henceforth he
spake of the fatherhood of God as if it
had to him a deeper sense than to most

[1] The rabbis use this expression, *Bath Kol*, for any
supernatural revelation. — ED.

of us Jews, though with us, as I have oft explained to thee, it is the central feeling of our faith.

Jesus did not remain long out in the wilderness with his cousin; he, indeed, early recognized his superiority, though he was his master and his teacher. For at the first the teaching of Jesus differed but in little from the teaching of Jochanan. He summed up his whole aim in the words which I had heard his followers use in the Temple: " Repent ye, for the kingdom of heaven is at hand;" and this he must have learnt from his cousin. So, too, like Jochanan, he mingled with the tax-gatherers and the soldiery, and above all addressed himself to the poor, and, as I was to see, exhorted the rich to distribute their possessions. In all these things he was but the follower of his cousin Jochanan. It is no wonder, therefore, that when Jesus separated himself from Jochanan, and began to be a teacher of men, many left Jochanan and followed after Jesus; and until this Jochanan met with a violent end at the hands of the rulers, there was in some sort a rivalry if not between the men themselves, at least between the followers of Jochanan and of Jesus.

But even from the first there was a difference in Jesus' manner of teaching, if not in the teaching itself. He, indeed, did not wait for men to come out to him in the wilderness, but returned to the towns and villages around the Sea of Galilee. Many of the fishermen left their work to follow him, and become, as he said, "fishers of men." He preached as before in the synagogues on the words of the prophets, but now he commenced to go forth to preach and teach among the people in their homes. Yet it was observed that he went not only among the rich and powerful, who are used in our country to receive all who come at meal-times, but most of all among the poor, and those despised of men for their ill life or their degraded occupations. Nor did he despise those who know not the Law nor keep its commands, but mixed freely with them, thereby incurring the wrath of those among us, and there are many, who are eager for the credit of the Law. Still, though he lived his life among the low and the vile, he practiced none of their ways, nor was aught of low or vile seen in him or those with him. Yet he turned against him many who would have been well disposed towards him, in that he followed his cousin's example, and spake kindly to the tax-gatherers and to the soldiers, whom the greater part of the Jews regard as the enemies of their country.

Now, as he began to live his life among the people, he began to do many signs and wonders, like all our great teachers and prophets. In truth, we say, how shall a man be accounted a prophet unless he can do wonders? Indeed, as Jesus himself said, "Why marvel ye at the signs? I give unto you an inheritance such as the whole world holds not." And the manner of his wonders was this: if a man was afflicted with a demon of madness, he would cause him to fix his eyes upon his, and after a while would speak sternly and suddenly to the demon within him, who would depart from him, rending his soul. So, too, would he do with women who were torn asunder by the demons fighting within. To these he would speak calmly after he had fixed their eyes, and,

behold, a great calm would come upon
them. But he used no exorcisms or magic
in his healing, nor spake he in the name
of God, but with the tone of one having
authority in himself. Hence many thought
he had within him a greater Daimon than
those afflicted men and women whom he
healed. Thence it was thought that for
this reason the demons of madness often
returned to those whom he had freed for
a while with greater violence after he had
gone forth from the place of their habita-
tion. There was much murmuring against
him for that he did his healing, not in the
name of God, but in his own name and his
own authority.

Yet he claimed no authority to decide
the questions of the Law; though many
applied to him in difficult cases, these he
referred to the learned in the Law, saying,
" Do ye as the scribes command." Yet
it was complained that he paid no great
attention to their commands himself, nor
for his followers. Nor did he rebuke men
when he saw them transgressing the Law
even in the greater transgressions. Thus
I have heard it said of him, that once with

his followers, he met a man laboring on the
Sabbath day, a sin which, according to the
Law, was punished with stoning.   But all
he said unto him was this: " Man, if thou
knowest what thou doest, blessed art thou ;
but if thou knowest not, accursed art thou,
and a transgressor of the Law." [1]   This is,
indeed, a dark saying.   Is each man, then,
to choose for himself which commands of
the Law he shall do, and which not?   The
fence of the Law, which our Sages have
built up with such labor and toil, would be
stricken down at one stroke.   Yet perhaps
in this he only followed the principle of our
Sages who have said, " The Sabbath was
made for you, not you for the Sabbath."

Such was the manner of life of this Jesus
up to the time when I first saw him in the
Temple.   Men knew not what to make of
him ; many regarded him as a prophet because of the signs and the wonders which
he did ; and those who were looking forward
to the blessed day in which Israel would be
free again under its own king hoped that
he was Elijah come again to prepare the
way for the new kingdom.

[1] This Logion is only found elsewhere in one MS. of
the Gospels, viz., in the Codex Bezæ at Cambridge. — ED.

III.

EARLIER TEACHING.

SERMON IN THE SYNAGOGUE OF THE
GALILÆANS.

III.

It must have been a year after I had first seen Jesus that I saw him again the second time in Jerusalem. It fell out in this wise: I was proceeding one morning to the meeting of the Sanhedrim, when, as I came near the Synagogue of the Galilæans in the Fish-Market, I found a crowd of men entering in. I asked one of them what was going forward, and he said, " Jesus the Nazarene will expound the Law." So I determined to take the morning service in this synagogue rather than with my colleagues in the Temple, and went in, the people giving way before me, as was my due as a member of the Sanhedrim.

Now, this synagogue of the Galilæans differed in naught from the rest of the synagogues of the Jews. It cannot be that thou hast not visited one of these when thou wast in the Holy City, but perchance thy memory is dim after all these years, and I will in a few words explain to thee

its arrangement. In the wall at the west
end was the cabinet containing the scrolls
of the Law, with a curtain before it, for
this is, as it were, the Holy of Holies of the
synagogue. The men go up to this, on to
the platform before it, by three steps. Then
comes a vacant space, in the midst of which
stands a dais, with a reading-desk whereon
the Law is read : this we call by your
Greek name *bema*. Then in the rest of
the hall sit the folk, arranged in benches
one after another, somewhat as in your
theatres. Now, as I came in, they had said
the morning psalms, and most of the Eighteen Blessings, and shortly after the reading of the Law began. The curtain was
drawn aside from the holy ark, the scroll of
the Law was taken thence, to the singing
of psalms unto the *bema*. Then, as is
customary, the messenger of the congregation summoned first to the reading of the
Law a Cohen, a descendant of Aaron, one
of the priestly caste. And after he had
read some verses of the Law in the holy
tongue, the dragoman read its translation
into Chaldee, so as to be understanded of
the unlearned folk, and of the women who

were in the gallery outside the synagogue, and separated from it by a grating. Then after the priest came a Levite, who also read some verses, and after him an ordinary Israelite. Then the messenger of the synagogue called out, " Let Rabbi Joshua ben Joseph arise." Then Jesus the Nazarene went up to the *bema* and read his appointed verses, and these were translated as before by the dragoman. And after the reading of the Law was concluded, the *Parnass*, or president of the congregation, requested Jesus to read the *Haphtara*, the lesson from the prophets; and this he did, using the cantillation with which we chant words of Holy Scripture. Yet never heard I one whose voice so thrilled me, and brought home to one the import of the great words; and this was strange, for his accent was, as I had before noticed, that of the Galilæan peasantry, at which we of Jerusalem were wont to scoff. Then, after the Law had been returned to the ark with song and psalm, Jesus turned round to the people on the *bema* and began his discourse. It is near five-and-twenty years since I heard him, and much have I forgotten in that long time. But many of his sayings still ring in my ears, and I will here put down, as far as possible in order, all that I can remember of the discourse.[1]

"It hath been written by the Prophet Esaias: Behold, his reward is with him, and his work before him. Yea, behold a man and his work before him. He that worketh not, let him not eat. Yet he that plougheth, let him plough in hope; he that thresheth, thresh in hope of partaking. Howbeit, he who longs to be rich is like a man who drinketh seawater: the more he drinketh the more thirsty he becomes, and never leaves off drinking till he perish. Blessed is he who also fasts that he may feed the poor: for it is more blessed to give than to receive. Yet let thy alms sweat into thy hands until thou know to whom thou givest. Where there are pains, thither hastens the physician: that which is weak shall be saved by that

---

[1] It must have been from a report of this discourse, and that given on p. 92, that the majority of those utterances of Jesus have been derived which are known in modern theology as "Agrapha." — ED.

which is strong. For the sake of the weak
I was weak, for the sake of the hungry I
hungered, for the sake of the thirsty I
thirsted. But woe to those who have yet
hypocritically taken from others; who are
able to help themselves, and yet wish to
take from others: for each man shall give
account in the day of judgment.

" That which thou hatest thou shalt not
do to another. Good things must come;
he is blessed through whom they come.
Love covereth a multitude of sins; so
never be joyful save when you look upon
your brother's countenance in love. Let
not the sun go down upon your wrath.
For the greatest of crimes is this: if a
man shall sadden his brother's spirit.
Blessed, too, are they who mourn for the
perdition of unbelievers. Do not give
occasion to the Wicked One. Who is the
Wicked One? He that tempts. Yet
none shall reach the kingdom of heaven
unless he have been tempted: for our
Father which is in heaven would rather
the repentance of a sinner than his correc-
tion. Yet he will cleanse the house of his
kingdom from all offence. Be, therefore,

careful and prudent and wise, lest any of
you be caught in the snares of the devil,
for that ancient enemy goes about buffet-
ing.

"If thou hast seen thy brother, thou
hast seen thy Lord, God the Father, whose
fatherland is everywhere, in heaven and
upon earth. Far and near, the Lord
knoweth his own. So grieve not the holy
spirit which is in you, nor extinguish the
light which shines in you. Guard the
flesh pure, and the signet spotless, so that
ye may take hold upon eternal life. For
our possessions are in heaven; therefore,
sons of men, purchase unto yourselves by
these transitory things which are not
yours, what is yours, and shall not pass
away."

I cannot tell thee, Aglaophonos, how
deeply this discourse affected me. Just as
the Hellenes are eager to find each day
some new beauty in man or the world, or
some new truth about the relation of
things, so we Hebrews rejoice in finding
new ideals in the relations of men. Each
of our Sages prides himself on this —

that he has said some maxim of wisdom
that none had thought of before him, and
so each of them is remembered in the
minds of men by one or more of his favorite maxims. But it is rare if in a whole
lifetime a sage sayeth more than one word
fit to be treasured up among men. Yet
was this man Jesus dropping pearls of
wisdom from his mouth in prodigal profusion. As each memorable word fell
from his lips, a murmur of delighted surprise passed round the synagogue, and
each man looked to his neighbor with
brightened eyes. Some of the thoughts,
indeed, I had heard from other of our
Sages, but never in so pointed a form,
surely never in such profusion from a
single sage.

And if what was said delighted us, the
manner in which it was said entranced
us still more. The voice of the speaker
answered to the thoughts he expressed, as
the Kinnor of David, according to our
Sages, turned the wind into music. When
he spoke of love, his voice was as the
cooing dove; when he denounced the oppressor, it clanged like a silver trumpet.

Indeed, his whole countenance and bearing changed in like manner, so that every
word he uttered seemed to be the outcome
of his whole being.

But most of all was it the vividness of
his eyes that impressed his words upon
us. I had seen them flashing with scorn
in the Temple, I now saw them melting
with tenderness in the synagogue; and
there was this of strange in them, that
they seemed to speak other and deeper
words. As he gazed upon us, I felt as if
all my inmost being was bare to the gaze
of those eyes. They seemed to know all
my secret thoughts and sins; and yet I
felt not ashamed, for as they saw the sins,
so they seemed to speak forgiveness of
them.

What I felt then, others felt with me,
for, as I afterwards learnt, each man felt
the same as the eyes of Jesus fell upon
him; and most curious it was that each
man thought as I did, that the eyes of the
speaker were upon him during the whole
of the discourse. I have seen here in Alexandria portraits of men painted by your
subtlest artists, in which, from whatever

place you looked at them, the eyes seemed to gaze upon you.   So was it with Jesus. Not alone did I, who was, as a member of the Sanhedrim, sitting immediately before him, feel his eyes pierce to my soul, but all who were in that synagogue felt the same. Nor did the effect die away after I had left the synagogue ; for days and days afterwards, whenever I closed my eyes, or gazed for long on the wall, I could see the eyes of Jesus, and with it his whole face, gazing upon me.

I had left the synagogue a little before the others, because a messenger had been sent from the Sanhedrim to seek for a member who should make up the quorum of Twenty-Three ; and this messenger, hearing that a member of the Sanhedrim was in the synagogue of the Galilæans, sent in to summon me.   When the sitting was over, I sought for Jesus again, but found that he had left the city.   And for a time I neither saw nor heard aught more of him, save such rumors as came to the Holy City from Galilee.   About this time many joined themselves unto him, going whithersoever he went.   Those,

too, who had joined themselves to Jochanan
passed over to him, for Jochanan had been
slain by Herod, whom he had rebuked for
his wicked living. It was, indeed, said
that Herod had also captured this Jesus
when he found that he was following in
the footsteps of Jochanan; but this proved
to be untrue, and the multitude thronged
more and more after Jesus, and from this
time he began to teach them regularly,
after the manner of our Sages. Yet he
did not pronounce decisions of Halacha
on questions of our Law; indeed, he dis-
claimed all interference with such questions. "I am not come," he said, "to take
away from the Law of Moses, nor to add
to the Law of Moses am I come." Only
one saying of his have I heard of wherein
he said aught at variance with the Torah.
When the children of a man who had recently died asked him in what way should
the property be divided, he said, "Let son
and daughter inherit alike." In this, as in
other things, he was more favorable to
the claims of the women than the Law
and the Sages. For this reason, perhaps,
it was that many women followed after

him, even joined in prayer with him and
those with him, against the custom of our
nation. Hence arose much scandal among
the more rigidly pious among us, who follow the saying of Joseph ben Jochanan,
" Engage not in much converse with
women." But I have heard naught of
evil that resulted from this free mingling
of men and women among his followers.
Yet Jesus was not against the due subordination of women, for he also said, " Let
the wife be in subordination to her husband."

Thou must know that among us our
Sages are of two kinds, the Halachists and
the Hagadists. The former deal with matters of the Law according to the tradition
they have received from their teacher; but
the latter expound the words of the
Scripture, and deal with the moral relations of man to man. Some of our Sages,
indeed, like the great Hillel, who died
when I was a child, have been equally
masters both of the Halacha and the
Hagada; and in many ways the teaching
of Jesus seems to have resembled, if it did
not follow, that of Hillel. I must tell thee

one anecdote about this Hillel which is
well known amongst us. He was distin-
guished for his evenness of temper, and
men would often in sport try to make him
lose it. A heathen came before him one
day, and declared that he would become
a Jew if only Hillel would tell him the
whole Law while he stood upon one foot,
hoping thereby to irritate Hillel by his presumption. But Hillel said only, "What
thou wilt not for thyself, do not to thy
neighbor. This is the whole of the Law;
all the rest is but commentary thereon.
Go and learn." Now, among the disciples of Hillel was one who compiled for
the heathen a summary of the Law in the
spirit of Hillel; and it seemed to me, from
what I heard of Jesus' teaching, that he
had learnt much from this summary, which
is called "The Two Ways." I will have
a copy written out for thee, for it is very
short.

Now, in all the teaching of Jesus which
I heard of about this time, he seems to
have expanded, but in no wise modified,
the teaching of "The Two Ways." Above
all, he seems to have warned men against

the evil feelings within, that lead to sins against the Law, and therein differed somewhat from the practice of our Sages, who think that by doing the Law and keeping to it rightful feelings shall grow, and evil thoughts fly away.

Yet while in many ways Jesus seemed to be of the School of Hillel, in others he cast in his lot with the men among us who claim to be especially favored of God, because — thou wilt smile, Aglaophonos — because they are poor. Thou hast read our Psalms, and knowest with what insistence the poor and the righteous, the rich and the wicked, are identified in them. Many of our nation have taken this to heart, and as it were pride themselves upon their humility, as some of them call themselves *Ebionim*, or the Poor; some, the *Zaddikim*, or Righteous; some, *Chasidim*, or Pious. Thou canst not call them a sect, for in a way they include the whole nation. In the Eighteen Blessings which form the staple of our daily prayers, the Lord is blessed as the Guardian and Refuge of the *Zaddikim*. Now, it was chiefly among these men, whether they called

themselves *Ebionim*, or *Zaddikim*, or
Chasidim, that Jesus found his chief adherents, though he seems to give his preference to the *Ebionim*, who have always
been insisting upon the blessedness of the
poor. Now, these men consider themselves
to be beyond all others the servants of the
Lord, and identify themselves with that
picture of the servant which has been
given by the Prophet Esaias. Thus in
all these ways Jesus appealed to the more
earnest part of our nation, and in him
were conjoined most of the movements
that had touched us most deeply. If any
had said at this time, " Jesus the Nazarene
is a follower of Jochanan the Baptizer, and
preaches ' The Two Ways ' to the Poor,"
none could have gainsaid him.

Yet all were wondering what he would
say to the other side of our nation's hopes.
The life of our nation had begun with a
deliverance ; our chief national feast recalls
that deliverance from Egypt to us every
year as the spring comes round. We have
become subject to all the great kingdoms
that have grown up round us, yet again and
again we have been delivered from each.

Thou and I have often wondered how it has come about that both Hellenes and Hebrews, who feel ourselves in different ways higher than these stolid Romans who rule us, have yet become subject to them. Thy nation hath acquiesced in their rule; my people never will. Every man who promises greatness among us is hoped for as the Deliverer. Many men about this time began to ask, Will Jesus the Nazarene be the Deliverer?

IV.

THE TWO WAYS.

IV.

Now, this is the "CATECHISM OF THE
TWO WAYS" which I have had copied out
for thee, for in it is the essence of the
teaching of Jesus, as he himself recognized in speaking to me, as thou wilt
shortly hear.

"There are two ways, one of life and
one of death, but there is a great difference between the two ways. Now, the
way of life is this: first, Thou shalt love
God who made thee; secondly, thy neighbor as thyself, and all things whatsoever
thou wouldest not should be done to thee,
do thou also not do to another. Thou
shalt not kill, thou shalt not commit adultery, thou shalt not corrupt boys, thou
shalt not commit fornication, thou shalt
not steal, thou shalt not use witchcraft,
thou shalt not use enchantments, thou
shalt not kill an infant whether before or
after birth, thou shalt not covet thy neighbor's goods.

" Thou shalt not forswear thyself, thou shalt not bear false witness, thou shalt not revile, thou shalt not bear malice.

" Thou shalt not be double-minded nor double-tongued ; for duplicity of tongue is a snare of death.

" Thy speech shall not be false nor vain.

" Thou shalt not be covetous, nor an extortioner, nor a hypocrite, nor malignant, nor haughty. Thou shalt not take evil counsel against thy neighbor.

" Thou shalt hate no man, but some thou shalt rebuke, and for some thou shalt pray, and some thou shalt love above thine own soul.

" My child, flee from all evil, and from all that is like unto it.

" Be not soon angry, for anger leadeth to murder ; nor given to party-spirit, nor contentious, nor quick-tempered, for from all these are generated murders.

" My child, be not lustful, for lust leadeth to fornication ; neither be a filthy talker, nor a lifter-up of the eyes, for from all these things are generated adulteries.

" My child, be not thou an observer of birds, for it leadeth to idolatry ; nor a charmer, nor an astrologer, nor a user of purifications; nor be thou willing to look on those things, for from all these is generated idolatry.

"My child, be not a liar, for lying leadeth to theft; nor a lover of money, nor fond of vainglory, for from all these things are generated thefts.

"My child, be not a murmurer, for it leadeth to blasphemy; neither self-willed, nor evil-minded, for from all these things are generated blasphemies.

"Be thou long-suffering, and merciful, and harmless, and quiet, and good, and trembling continually at the words which thou hast heard.

"Thou shalt not exalt thyself, nor shalt thou give presumption to thy soul. Thy soul shall not be joined to the lofty, but with the just and lowly shalt thou converse.

"The events that happen to thee shalt thou accept as good, knowing that without God nothing taketh place.

"My child, thou shalt remember night and day him that speaketh to thee the word of God.

" But thou shalt seek out day by day the faces of the saints, that thou mayest rest in their words.

" Thou shalt not desire division, but shalt make peace between those at strife ; so thou shalt judge justly. Thou shalt not respect a person in rebuking for transgressions.

" Thou shalt not be of two minds whether it shall be or not.

" Be not one that stretcheth out his hands to receive, but shutteth them close for giving.

" If thou hast, thou shalt give with thine hands a ransom for thy sins.

" Thou shalt not hesitate to give, nor when thou givest shalt thou murmur, for thou shalt know who is the good recompenser of the reward.

" Thou shalt not turn away from him that needeth, but shalt share all things with thy brother, and shalt not say that they are thine own; for if ye are fellow-sharers in that which is imperishable, how much more in perishable things.

" Thou shalt not take away thine hand from thy son or from thy daughter, but from their youth up shalt thou teach them the fear of God.

" Thou shalt not in thy bitterness lay commands on thy man-servant or thy maid-servant, who hope in the same God, lest they should not fear him who is God over you both; for He cometh not to call men according to the outward appearance, but to those whom the Spirit hath prepared.

" But ye, servants, shall be subject to your masters as to a figure of God in reverence and fear.

" Thou shalt hate all hypocrisy, and everything which is not pleasing to the Lord.

" Thou shalt not forsake the commandments of the Lord, but shalt keep what thou hast received, neither adding thereto nor taking away from it.

" Thou shalt confess thy transgressions, and shalt not come to thy prayer with an evil conscience. This is the way of life.

" But the way of death is this. First of all, it is evil and full of curse; murders, adulteries, lusts, fornications, thefts, idolatries, witchcrafts, sorceries, robberies, false-

witnessings, hypocrisies, double-hearted-
ness, deceit, pride, wickedness, self-will,
covetousness, filthy talking, jealousy, presumption, haughtiness, flattery.

"Persecutors of the good, hating truth,
loving a lie, not knowing the reward of
righteousness, not cleaving to that which
is good nor to righteous judgment, watch-
ing not for the good but for the evil, far
from whom is meekness and patience, loving vain things, seeking after reward, not
pitying the poor, not toiling with him who
is vexed with toil, not knowing Him that
made them, murderers of children, destroy-
ers of the image of God, turning away
from him that is in need, vexing him that
is afflicted, advocates of the rich, lawless
judges of the poor, wholly sinful.

"Take heed that no one make thee to
err from this way of teaching, since he
teacheth thee not according to God."

V.

THE WOMAN TAKEN IN ADULTERY.
THE RICH YOUNG MAN.

V.

It must have been many months after I had heard him discourse in the Galilæan synagogue that I again saw Jesus the Nazarene. We in Jerusalem had our own concerns to think of.

At this time the long monopoly of rule by the Sadducees was gradually being broken. Of the three divisions of the Sanhedrim, that of the ordinary Israelites had become almost entirely composed of the Pharisees; I myself had been elected as one of that party, and even in the other two sections of the Priests and of the Levites, many, especially among the latter, held with the Pharisees. Nor was this without influence upon the political issues of the times. The Sadducees, being the sacerdotal party, had no cause why they should be dissatisfied with the position they held in the State under the Romans; but we of the Pharisees felt far otherwise about the national hopes for deliverance.

Since my days the influence of the Pharisees has become predominant in the
nation, and I foresee that the struggle
between us and the Romans cannot be
delayed for long. At the time of which
I am writing, the hegemony had not yet
passed over to the Pharisees, and it was
of import for us all to know whether any
man of influence was on our side, or on
that of the Sadducees, or whether he cared
for neither, and cast in his lot with the
smaller sects.

Now, it happened about this time that I
was attending my place in the Sanhedrim
of Israelites, to judge of a case of adultery.
But in this matter our Sages, and especially those of the Pharisaic tradition, had
made great changes in the Law as laid
down for us by Moses; for he, as thou
knowest, commands that a woman taken
in adultery shall be stoned to death. Now,
for a long time among us there has been
an increasing horror of inflicting the
death penalty. If a Sanhedrim inflicts
capital punishment more than once in
seven years, it is called a Sanhedrim of
murderers. Yet the Law of Moses de-

clared that whosoever was guilty of adultery would be put to death. What, then, was to be done? It is against the principle of justice that any should be punished for an offence of which he is ignorant. Hence, in capital offences, our Sages, to mercy inclined, have laid it down that a man must be assumed to be ignorant of the guilt of the offence, unless it be proved that he had been solemnly warned of its gravity; and in our Law proof can only be given by two simultaneous witnesses. Hence it is impossible to obtain conviction for a woman who hath committed adultery, unless proof is given that she hath been previously warned by two persons at once. This can scarcely ever be. No Jewish woman in my time has ever been stoned as the Law commands for this sin. Some think that this is too great a leniency, and of evil result for the morality of the folk.

When I arrived at the hall of polished stones near the Temple, in which the Sanhedrim holds its sittings, the trial had nearly come to a conclusion. The inquiry had been made if any two credible wit-

nesses had given the woman the preliminary caution, and none answering to the
call, it remained only for the *Ab Beth Din*,
the president of the court, to dismiss the
prisoner with the words of caution and
advice which are customary on such
occasions : " My daughter, perhaps thou
wert led into sin by too much wine, or by
thoughtlessness, or perhaps by thy youth;
perchance it was mixing in crowds, or
wicked companions that led thee to sin:
go, and for the sake of the great Name,
do not bring it to pass that thou must be
destroyed by the water of jealousy."   And
with these words the court was dismissed,
and several of us were appointed to take
the woman to her home, and induce the
man, her husband, to take her to him once
again.   Now, as we were passing through
the courts of the Temple, we saw Jesus
the Nazarene in one of the smaller courts,
seated, teaching the people, some of whom
sat at his feet.   But it seemed to some of
us a favorable opportunity to test what he
would say as regards the Law of Moses
relating to adultery : for if he would declare
that the Law must be carried out in all its

rigor, that would show that our Sages were
more merciful than he; if, on the other
hand, he adopted the opinion of our Sages,
that would in so far commit him to support
their attitude towards the Law in general.
In any case, it seemed a suitable occasion
to test his power of dealing with the Law,
and it is customary among us to put such
test cases before the younger Sages.

We therefore turned aside and entered
into the smaller court, and all rose to do
honor to the Sanhedrim. Then one of us
said to him, " Rabbi, this woman was taken
in adultery, in the very act. Now, Moses
in the Law hath commanded that such
should be stoned: what sayest thou ? "
Now, when the man told him that the
woman had been taken in the very act of
adultery, a deep blush passed over his face,
and he turned his eyes downwards. Then
he bent down to the ground, hiding his
face altogether from us, and writing, as it
were, something on the sand of the floor.
Now, at first, I thought of the cry of the
money-changers that I had heard, and felt
ashamed in my soul that such a question
should be brought before this man, of all

men : for our Sages have said, " The greatest of sins is this — to bring a blush upon
thy neighbor's face in public." But the
others thought not of this, but once more
they asked him, " Rabbi, what sayest thou
shall be done in this case ? " Then, without raising his head, Jesus said in a low
tone, " Let him among you that is without
sin cast the first stone." Then we saw that
his shame had been for us, and for our
want of feeling in putting such a question
in the very presence of her who had sinned.
And in this matter we hold that sin can
be in thought as well as in act, and which
of us could say that we were without sin
even in thought ? So, in very shame, we
turned and went, and left Jesus alone with
the woman.

Yet, after we had come away from him,
Matathias ben Meshullam said, " That is
well, — we are rightly rebuked; but yet,
dost thou not see that this man hath not
answered our question, nor do we know, as
we wished, what attitude he takes towards
the carrying out of the Law ? I hear that
each morning he preaches to the people in
the Temple. Let us now tomorrow

put such questions to him that he cannot evade, and find out to which of our
parties he belongs; for this is a man that
is getting great weight with the people,
and it imports us to know where he stands
with regard to us." So it was determined
among us that the next morning a Sadducee and a Pharisee should put to him
queries which should determine what views
he held on the great questions which dis-
tinguished the two great parties of the
State.

But that very afternoon I was to learn
that this Jesus had to deal with questions
with which none of our parties concerned
themselves. For, as I was coming near to
Gethsemane, I met Jesus with a band of
men and women going out towards Bethany, and I passed them with the salutation
of " Peace." But as I passed, a young
man whom I knew, that had recently come
into great possessions upon the death of
his father, came up and asked, " Who is
that man whom thou hast just greeted ? "
and I said, " Jesus the Nazarene." Then,
suddenly, he set off running to catch them
up, and being curious, I turned and fol-

lowed him. When I reached them I found
the young man kneeling before Jesus, gazing up to him, and he said, " Good Master,
I have inherited great possessions; what
shall I do that I may inherit the life everlasting?" Jesus said to him, " Call not me
'Good;' none is good but the One. If
thou wouldest enter into life, do the commandments." The young man asked,
" Which?" Jesus said, using the doctrine
of "The Two Ways," "Do not kill, do not
commit adultery, do not steal, do not bear
false witness, do not defraud, honor thy
father and thy mother, and love thy neighbor as thyself." Then the young man
said, " All these things have I kept from
my youth up: what lack I yet?" Then
Jesus said, " One thing thou lackest: go
thy way, sell all thou hast, and give unto
the poor, and thou shalt have heavenly
treasures: come then and follow me."
The young man began to scratch his head,
and seemed in doubt. Then Jesus said
unto him, " How is it thou canst say, 'I
have done the Law and the Prophets,'
since it is written in the Law, 'Thou shalt
love thy neighbor as thyself'? Behold,

many of thy brothers, sons of Abraham,
are clothed but in dung, and die for hunger, while thy house is full of many goods,
and there goeth not forth aught from it
unto them." But the young man rose, and
went away in sorrow and confusion. Then
Jesus looked round upon those who were
there, and said, " How hard it is for them
that trust in riches to enter into the kingdom of God! It is easier for an elephant
to go through a needle's eye, as the saying
is, than for a rich man to enter into the
kingdom of God." Then a murmur arose
among all those present, and they began
to move on, and I left them. And I said
to myself, " This man is neither Pharisee,
nor Sadducee, nor Herodian ; these be the
thoughts of the Ebionim."

VI.

THE TESTINGS IN THE TEMPLE.

VI.

Now, on the morrow, many of us who had agreed together to test the opinions of this Jesus went to the Temple and found Jesus walking in the corridors. Then he that was of most authority among us said unto Jesus, " Rabbi, we would ask certain questions of thee ; " and Jesus answered, " Ask, and it shall be answered unto thee."

Thou must know that among us Jews there be two chief schools of thought, or rather thou mightest say, parties of the State. The one holds with the High Priest and the rulers, and is mainly made up of those whom ye Hellenes call the Best, and their retainers. These be known as the Sadducees, for their leaders are mainly of the family of the High Priest Sadduk. Now, the other party is in some sort the party of the Demos, in that they seek to lessen the power of the High Priests and their families. But with us, as thou knowest, all things turn upon reli-

gion, and this second party differ chiefly
from the Sadducees, for that they are more
in earnest with the matters of the Law,
and chiefly they fear the influence of thy
nation, Aglaophonos, in drawing the Israelite away from the Law. Therefore have
they increased precept upon precept, so as
to make, as they say, a fence round the
Law. And as they would separate themselves from the heathen by this fence, they
call themselves Pharisees, that is, Separa-
tists.

Now, it was nowise easy to learn whether
a man was of the one party or the other.
For he might be eager for the Law, and so
be Pharisaic in color, and yet approve of
the dominion of the priests, and thus be
a Sadducee. Yet in one chief matter of
thought they went asunder contrariwise,
and that was concerning the resurrection
of the dead. Now, with regard to that,
the Sadducees held that naught was said
in the Law of Moses, and therefore no son
of Israel need concern himself with it. But
the Pharisees, on the other hand, laid great
weight upon this. So here was a touch-
stone by which to learn whether this Jesus

followed the one or the other of the two great divisions of our nation.

Then, as was agreed upon, Kamithos the Sadducee came forward to ask him the question which should determine whether he held with them that there was no resurrection from the dead, or with the rest of the nation. He said, " Rabbi, it is written in the Torah, if brethren dwell together, and one of them die and have no son, the wife of the dead one shall not marry without, unto a stranger; her husband's brother shall take her to him to wife, and raise up seed unto his brother. Suppose, now, there are seven brethren, and the first takes a wife, and dying leaves no son; and the second takes her, as is our custom, and dies without leaving any seed; and the third likewise, and so on, till the whole seven had married her, and yet had no son; then the woman dies also: when they shall rise from the dead together, whose wife shall she be of them? for all seven had her to wife." And Jesus answered and said, "Ye are at fault, and know not the Scriptures, nor the power of God; for in the resurrection they neither

marry, nor are given in marriage, but are
even as the angels which are in heaven.
And as an indication from Scripture that
the dead rise, is it not written in the book
of Moses, when God spake to him from
the bush, saying, ' I am the God of Abraham, and the God of Isaac, and the God
of Jacob'? He is not the God of the
dead, but the God of the living: therefore
are ye in error."

And we were surprised at the subtlety
of the man; and chiefly men marvelled at
the wisdom of this man in finding what
we call a support, that is, a text of Scripture on which to hang the doctrine of the
life after death, which many believe to
have grown up among us since the sacred
Scriptures were written: for in them little,
if anything, was said of the world to come.
Now, Jesus in his answer had happened
upon a text which said that Abraham and
Isaac and Jacob were living when they
were dead to this world, and the people
marvelled greatly thereat.

Now, it had been agreed upon, that
after the Sadducees had asked their question and been answered, I should stand

forth and test this man Jesus on behalf of
the Pharisees. Now, one of our Sages
hath said, "Be as careful of a little precept as of a great one;" whereas our great
master Hillel had, as I have told thee,
summed up the whole Law in one precept,
"Love thy neighbor as thyself." Therefore, we of the Pharisees wished to know
whether this Jesus agreed with the one
sage or the other; so I spake unto him
and said, "Rabbi, which is the first commandment, by doing which I shall inherit
the life everlasting?" But at first he answered me not directly, but said, "How
readest thou?" Then I remembered me
the words of the "Catechism of the Two
Ways," and answered, "Thou shalt love
the Lord thy God with all thy heart, and
with all thy strength, and with all thy
mind, and thy neighbor as thyself: whatsoever thou wouldest not for thyself, do
not to another." And he said unto me,
"Thou hast answered right; and the first
of the commandments is the *Shema :*
'Hear, O Israel; the Lord thy God is
one God.' And the second is like, namely
this: 'Thou shalt love thy neighbor as

thyself.' There is none other commandment greater than these. This do, and
thou shalt live." Then I was rejoiced,
and said unto him, "Well, Rabbi, thou
hast said the truth: there is one God, and
there is none other but him; and to love
him with all the heart, and with all the
understanding, and with all the soul, and
all the strength, and to love one's neighbor
as one's self, is more than all the burnt
offerings and sacrifices." Then Jesus became gracious unto me, and said, " Thou
art not far from the kingdom of God."

But then I would learn further from this
man who spake so well, and ask him the
question which is current in our schools
on this subject, and I said to him, " But,
Rabbi, who is my neighbor?" and he
answered with a *mashal*, or parable, and
said, "To what is the matter like? A
certain man was going down from Jerusalem to Jericho; and he fell among robbers, which both stripped him and beat
him, and departed, leaving him half dead.
And by chance a certain priest was going
down that way: and when he saw him, he
passed by on the other side. And in like

manner a Levite also, when he came to
the place, and saw him, passed by on the
other side. But a certain Israelite,[1] as
he journeyed, came where he was : and
when he saw him, he was moved with
compassion, and came to him, and bound
up his wounds, pouring on them oil and
wine ; and he set him on his own beast,
and brought him to an inn, and took care
of him. And on the morrow he took out
two pence, and gave them to the host, and
said, 'Take care of him; and whatsoever
thou spendest more, I, when I come back
again, will repay thee.' Which of these
three, thinkest thou, proved neighbor unto
him that fell among the robbers ? " Then
I said, " Not the priest, nor the Levite,
though they held office in Israel, but the
simple Israelite who showed mercy upon
him." Then Jesus said unto me, " Go and
do thou likewise ;" and at this moment we
were all summoned to the mid-day sacrifice in the Temple.

When Jesus had departed, after the sacrifice, we all met together and discussed
his answers, which had stamped him in

---

[1] The gospel version reads " Samaritan." — ED.

our minds as a master in the art of question and answer, which is with us as favorable a trial of skill as oratory or poetry
with you Hellenes. Now, as regards the
question of the Sadducees, men thought
he had spoken more openly; for though
he had evaded a direct answer to the
question of the seven brothers and their
wife, he had yet implied that they all
would have a part in the life to come.
Some regretted that the question had not
been put differently, and the problem set
— if a son had been born through the
seventh brother: for this might have
thrown light upon the question of the
schools, whether the brother's widow was
to be still regarded as his wife if seed had
been raised to him after his death. But
as to the support which Jesus had taken
from Scripture for the life everlasting,
though here again he had answered question by question, it was decided that he
was against the Sadducees on this point.

But on the questions which I had put
to him, all had agreed that he had answered as a Pharisee, even as Hillel might
have answered, for he had yea-said the

doctrine which I had cited from the beginning of " The Two Ways " in which the
doctrine of Hillel is summed up; and even
as to my further question, as to who is the
chaber, or neighbor, though opinions were
divided, most thought that he had spoken
as a Pharisee might have spoken: for
thou knowest, Aglaophonos, that our nation is divided into three great classes — ·
the *Cohanim*, or Priests; the Levites;
and the common Israelites. Now, of these,
the two former are the officials of the
Temple, and most if not all of the Sadducees are from this class. And, in declaring himself on the side of the third
class of simple Israelites, Jesus had, we all
thought, declared himself on the side of
the Pharisees.

VII.

THE SECOND SERMON.

VII.

I CANNOT clearly remember at what season of the year it was that I next saw Jesus; indeed, I am surprised to think that, after the lapse of nearly five-and-twenty years, I can still remember almost all that passed on the various occasions when I was in his presence. Yet I think it was about the time of the feast which we hold in memory of the rededication of the Temple under the Maccabæans that I again saw and heard the Galilæan stranger; for I mind me that I had just been taking the eight-branch candlestick which we use in the ceremonials of this feast to Petachayah the silversmith to be mended, when on my return I saw a throng collected round the synagogue of the Galilæ-ans, and entering in, found that Jesus was to preach that day. The same ceremonial was gone through as I have already described to thee: the Law was taken from the ark with rejoicing; priest and Levite and four ordinary Israelites were summoned to hear it read, and again the crier called, "Let Rabbi Joshua, the son of Rabbi Joseph, arise." Now, it chanced that this time, I, as a member of the Sanhedrim, was summoned to the reading of the Law immediately after Jesus, and for a time, as is customary, we stood together upon the *bema*. I observed that, as the reading of the Law proceeded, the eyes of the Nazarene became fixed upon the ark, and a veil of mysterious tenderness seemed to come over them, as if he were in communion with the *Shechinah*, or Glory, itself. It seemed to me that afterwards, when he read the *Haphtara* from the prophets, and when he preached, something remained in him of this mystical communion.

Perhaps it was for this that we seemed to miss that sense of individual address which we had before observed in his eyes. No longer did these speak to us other and deeper thoughts than the words of the preacher; they seemed to dream of divine things, and so caused us also to be rapt in mystic musings. I cannot on this ac-

count recall for you all or even many of
the words which he uttered on this occasion. He began with some plain teaching
about practice. Soon he went on to speak
of himself in a marvellous way, as if he
would imply that communion with him
and with the Most High were one and the
same, and then in his last words he seemed
to speak of the Last Things. And here
again his words seemed as if he identified
himself with the great Judge.

Now, this is not so strange to our mode
of thinking in Israel as thou mightest
think. Almost all our prophets speak the
oracles of God as if they were using the
very words of the Lord. Thou canst read
in the Greek translation of the Seventy
many passages of the prophets in which
the very words of the Lord are given.
Yet in most, if not all, cases the prophet
beginneth, " Thus saith the Lord," or end-
eth, " This is the word of the Lord." But
with this Jesus it was otherwise. He
spoke as the ancient prophets do, but
whether from his rapt intentness in the
message he was delivering, or because he
felt his spirit for the time merged in the

divine, he spoke as if the message was his.
And as he spoke, I saw looks of amaze-
ment pass between many in the synagogue, and one old graybeard rose as if to
protest, and then, shaking his withered
hands above his head, went out of the
synagogue.

I will here set down for thee as many of
the words that fell from Jesus' lips on this
occasion as I can remember. They are
but few, but many of them are weighty,
and I have told thee above the general
lines of thought which seemed to run
through his discourse; and these are the
words as far as I remember them.[1]

"Cultivate faith and hope, through
which is born that love of God and man
which gives the eternal life. Those are
the sons of God who walk in the spirit of
God. What you preach before the folk,
do in deed before every one. Accept not
anything from any man, and possess not
anything in this world. For the Father
wisheth to be given to each man from his
own gifts. Cleave unto the saints: for

[1] See note on p. 42. — Ed.

they that cleave unto them shall be sancti-
fied. Yet shall there be schisms and here-
sies: for there is a shame which leadeth
to death, as there is a shame which leadeth to life. Is it not enough for the disciples to be as the Master? If in a little
you are not faithful, who shall give unto
you what is much? Seek the great, and
the little will be added to you; seek the
heavenly, and the things of earth will be
superadded.

" He that wonders shall reign, he who
reigns shall find rest. My secret is for
me, and for those that are mine are the
things which eye saw not, and ear heard
not, which entered not into the heart of
man, whatsoever things God prepared for
them that love him. Those who wish to
see me, and wish to cling to the kingdom,
must take me through affliction and suffering. For he that is near me is near the
fire, he that is far from me is far from the
kingdom. Where one is, there too am I;
where twain are, there too will I be. As
any of you sees himself in the water or in
the mirror, so let him see me in himself.

" They that love me shall receive the

crown.   I will choose me the good, those good whom my Father in the heavens hath given me.   Let the lawless continue in lawlessness, the just be justified.   Behold, I make the last as the first, and all things new.   In whatsoever state I find you, in that also will I judge you."

Never heard I any who spoke of himself as this man did.   For days and days afterwards some of his words came to me again and again.   Whenever I was alone I seemed to hear his voice saying, " Where one is, there too am I; where twain are, there too will I be."   Whenever I gazed on the running stream or looked on the polished steel of the mirror, again I seemed to hear him say, "As any of you sees himself in the water or in the mirror, so let him see me in himself."   And, in truth, at times my features seemed to fade away, and the face of Jesus gaze upon me.

Others thought not as I.   When we assembled after the sermon, to talk over it, as is our custom, I found that most had been chiefly touched by certain sayings at the end of the sermon, in which Jesus seemed to speak of the future life and the last judgment. Thou knowest, Aglaophonos, that with regard to these matters I incline more to the teaching of the Sadducean sect, who hold that Holy Scripture speaketh not of these things, and that, therefore, we need not and should not think thereon. But there were few who held that doctrine in the synagogue that day, and these thought most of the words in which Jesus seemed to claim the prerogatives of the Divine Judge. " I was amazed," quoth Serachyah ben Pinchas, " when he spoke of judging us himself in the last days : it wanted but a little that I had rent my garments at the blasphemy. But surely, thought I to myself, the man will shortly tell us, ' These are the words of the Lord,' and so I refrained."

Now I will tell thee of a most strange event that happened with me and this Jesus. A day or two after this, I was sitting in my room and studying the words of Torah, and had fallen into deep thought on the things of this life and the next, and gradually I fell thinking of certain words that I had heard from Jesus the Nazarene, as I have before told you. Hast thou ever felt, Aglaophonos, as if some one was gazing upon thee, and thou couldst not refrain from looking round to see who it was? So I felt at this moment, and I looked up from the sacred scroll, and lo! Jesus the Nazarene stood before me, gazing upon me with those piercing eyes I can never forget. His face was pale and indistinct, but the eyes shone forth as if with tenderness and pity. Then he seemed to lean forward, and spoke to me in a low yet piercing voice these words: "Awake thou that sleepest, and arise from the dead, and the Christ shall shine upon thee." I had shrunk back from his gaze, and was, indeed, in all amaze and wonder that he should be in the room; but when I looked again, behold, he was gone, there was no man there.

But this is not all the wonder of that event, for, being startled, and, indeed, somewhat fearful at his sudden appearance and disappearance, I arose and went out into the highway, and went out to walk on the Gethsemane road. Now, as I came clear of the city, I saw a group of

men coming down the opposite hill, and
when they came near, behold, it was Jesus
and some of his friends. I was astonished
and surprised beyond all measure, for how
could Jesus have just been with me, and
be now coming from Gethsemane? And
when they were passing me, Jesus glanced
at me very slightly, as at a stranger — he
that had spoken to my soul but a few
minutes since.

Now, after they had passed me, there
came one running after them whom I knew
— one Meshullam ben Hanoch — and I
stopped him and asked him whither he
was going, and he said, "Stay me not.
I have run all the way from Bethany to
catch up that man thou seest there, Jesus
the Nazarene;" and with that he took up
his running and left me.

I knew not what to think. I had seen
and heard Jesus in my own house in Jerusalem, and lo! at that very same time, as
I now learned, he had been at Bethany.
What thinkest thou, Aglaophonos, — can
a man be in two places at one and the
same time? or can it be that the mind of
man, and the power of his eye, can go

forth from his body and create a vision of another man that hath all the semblance of reality? I know not what to think; but I have heard that, even after his death, those who were nearest and dearest to Jesus saw him and heard him even as I did. Nor do I wonder at this, after what has occurred to myself.

VIII.

THE REBUKING OF JESUS.

VIII.

Now, it chanced that about this time I was invited to a feast at the house of Elisha ben Simeon, one of the leaders of the Pharisees in Jerusalem. His son had become thirteen years old that week, and, as is our custom, was received into the holy congregation as a Son of the Covenant on the Sabbath. He had been summoned up to the reading of the Law, and had himself read aloud a portion of it; for from this day onward he was to be treated in all matters of religion as if he were a man. Being a friend of his father, I had attended his synagogue, and heard the lad's pure voice for the first time in his life declare publicly his faith in the Most High.

After the service in the synagogue, his friends accompanied the father and the lad to their house, and with them went I, who had known the father from our schoolboy days, and the little lad from the time of his birth.

Now, it chanced that, as we came near the door of Elisha's house, we met Jesus the Nazarene, and two or three with him. So Elisha greeted them, and invited them courteously to join the feast, as is the custom among us. And Jesus and the others assented, and followed into the house with us. "To table, to table!" cried Elisha, pointing to the couches standing round the well-filled board.

When we were all seated, the host and his son came round with an ewer and basin to perform the washing of the hands prescribed by the Law. But when they came to the Galilæan strangers, these refused, saying, "We wash not before meals."

"Then we must serve ye last," said Elisha, with a smile. But the others took not the matter so pleasantly; for since we have one common dish, which is handed round to the guests for them to take their food with their fingers, it is considered gross ill-breeding for a man not to perform the ceremony of washing before meals.

Then Elisha took a seat at the centre of the table, and said the grace before meals. Then he broke bread, and, dipping a morsel into salt for each of the guests, he called his son to him to carry it round. When he saw that each of the guests had a piece of bread dipped in salt, Elisha recited the blessing on the bread, "Blessed art Thou, O Lord our God, who bringest forth bread from the earth," and all said "Amen." And one of the guests said to Elisha, "I am glad we are not in Babylon."

"How so, Phineas?" said Elisha to the man, who was well known at all feasts at that time in Jerusalem.

And Phineas said, "For there they only eat bread with their bread."

"Nay, that would not suit thee, Phineas. Thou art no Nazarite;" and most of the guests who knew him laughed.

Then Elisha clapped his hands, and the slaves took round the first course of salted fish; then afterwards the cold baked meats — for, being the Sabbath, the food had been prepared the day before.

Then one of the guests said to one of the Galilæans, "Is it true that you allow fowl to be boiled in milk in your country?"

"Yes, truly; why not?" said the Galilæan.

"Is it not written thrice in the Law," said the guest, "'Thou shalt not seethe the kid in its mother's milk'?"

"In our country," said the Galilæan, "fowls give no milk." And we all of us laughed, save only Jesus.

"Nay, but the Sages have carried their prohibition even unto fowls, lest the people be led to confuse flesh and flesh."

By this time we had arrived at the third and last course of salted olives, lettuces, and radishes. And again the bowl and ewer were passed round, and this time the Galilæans did not refuse the water. Then the new son of the covenant recited in his clear voice the grace after meals. And all rose, while the slaves removed the remnants. Then said Elisha, "It is not well that when so many are together we should depart without discussing some words of the Law. My little Lazarus here would fain learn some new thing from the many learned men present on this day of his being received into Israel."

"Well, then," said one of the company, "I should like to put a question to our friends here from Galilee." And they said, "Speak, Rabbi."

And he addressed himself to Jesus, and said, " Why walk not thy disciples according to the tradition of the elders, but eat bread with unwashen hands ? "

Then Jesus spoke out, and as he spoke he strode up and down the room, with his hand clutching the air, and the vein throbbing on his left temple. " Well hath Esaias prophesied of you hypocrites, as it is written, ' This people honoreth me with their lips, but their heart is far from me. Howbeit in vain do they worship me, teaching for doctrines the commandments of men.' " Then facing us all, he added, " For ye lay aside the commandment of God, and hold the tradition of men."

" How so, master? " said Elisha; " prove thy words."

" It is said in the Word of God, ' Honor thy father and thy mother,' and yet the Sages say, ' If a man be asked by his father or mother to honor them with a gift, and he say, " I vow that thing to the Almighty," then it is *Corban*,' and put aside for the Lord, so that his parents cannot enjoy thereof. Thus by your tradition about vows ye make the Word of God

concerning honor to parents of none effect, and many like things ye do."

Then Elisha said, " But the Sages are
by no means at one in that matter of the
vows, and in particular many of them declare all the vows annulled that would
work against our duty to our parents, or
even against our love to our neighbor.
Yet, even if we take the more stricter tradition, in what manner that absolves us
from washing our hands before meals, I
see not."

" Nay, it is the same thing," replied
Jesus.   " Ye Pharisees make clean the
outside of the cup and platter, but your
inward thoughts are full of ravening and
wickedness.   Ye fools! did not the Holy
One, blessed be He, who made that which
is without, make also that which is within?
Therefore give for alms that which is
within, kindly thoughts and friendly feelings.   If ye do that, all things are clean
unto you."

Then I said unto Jesus, for this matter
touched us scribes nearly, " Master, in
speaking thus against tradition thou re-
proachest us also that be scribes."

And he answered, "Woe, woe unto ye, scribes! which desire to walk in long robes, and love greetings in the markets, and the higher seats in the synagogues, and the chief places at feasts, which devour widows' houses, and for a show make long prayers."

Then an angry murmur rose among all the folk there assembled at the harsh words of the stranger, when suddenly was heard the voice of Simeon ben Lazarus, the father of Elisha, a very old man, who sat in the corner and said : —

"Young man, fourscore years and two have I lived upon this earth; a Pharisee have I been from the day I became a son of the covenant, like little Lazarus there; a scribe was I during all the working days of my life. I did what the Law and the Sages command, yet never thought I in so doing of men's thoughts or praises. Surely, if the Lord command, a good Jew will obey. And as in many things, many acts of this life, the Law speaketh not in plain terms, surely we should follow the opinion of those who devote all their life to the study of the Law.

"I have never sought the praises of men, their greetings or their honors, in obeying the Law.   In all that I have done I have sought one thing — to fulfil the will of our Father which is in heaven.

"As for what thou sayest, that inward thought and outward act should go together in the service of God and man, that is a verity, and often have I heard the saying from the great Hillel — may his memory be for a blessing!   But if outward act may be clean when inward thought may be unclean, how, on the other hand, can we know the purity of what is within, except it be decided by the cleanliness of what is without?   How, above all, shall we teach our little ones, like my Lazarus there, to feel what is good and seemly, except by first teaching them to do the acts that are seemly and good?

"And as for what thou sayest as to the hypocrisy of us Pharisees and scribes, I say unto thee, — and in a few days I must see the face of my Maker, — I say unto thee, I have known many an Ebionite, which thou seemest to be, who was well spoken within, but ill doing without.   So,

too, I have known many a scribe and
many a Pharisee who neither carried their
good deeds on their shoulders, nor said,
' Wait, I have to finish some godly deed ; '
nor set off their good deeds against their
sins ; nor boasted of their sacrifices for
godly works ; nor did they seek out their
sins that they might pay for them by their
virtues ; nor were they Pharisees from fear
of the Divine punishment. They were
Pharisees from love of the Lord, and did
throughout their life what they knew to
be his commands."

But Jesus spoke gently unto the old
man, and said naught but, " Nay, master, I
spoke not of thee, nor of men like thee.
These be the true Pharisees ; the rest but
have the Pharisaic color."

" That is so," said old Simeon. " I
have heard what King Jannaus said :
' Fear not the Pharisees, nor those who
are no Pharisees ; but fear the colored
ones, who are only Pharisees in appearance, who do the deeds of Zimri and de-
mand the rewards of Phineas.' "

But before the old man could finish.
there was a movement at the doorway,

and a high, thin voice cried out, " Where is this kidnapper of souls? where is this filcher of young lives? where is Jesus the Nazarene ? "

" Behold me," said Jesus, turning towards the voice; and an old man, with the rent garment of the mourner, and with hair all distraught, came up to the Nazarene with arms outstretched and clutching fingers.

" Give me my son, my Elchanan ! " he cried. " Thou hast taken him from me last Passover, saying, ' Father and mother, yea, all that a man hath, shall he give up to follow me.' He left me to follow thee; what hast thou done with him ? — my Elchanan ! my Elchanan ! "

" He died, and is at peace."

" Then give him back to me again. Thou canst do all things, men say : make whole the sick, let see the blind, cause the lame to walk, and give peace to the troubled mind. Give me, then, back my Elchanan thou hast taken from me."

" There is One alone that can quicken the dead," said Jesus, and walked sternly past him.

IX.

JESUS IN THE TEMPLE.

IX.

But a few days after what I have nar-
rated to thee, I had attended a full meeting
of the Sanhedrim in the hall of hewn stones
in the Priests' Court of the Temple. When
the session was over, we went forth, and,
turning to the right, passed into the Court
of the Israelites, and so through Nicanor's
Gate into the Court of the Women. Now,
as we went down the fifteen steps that lead
into this court, we could see, through the
Beautiful Gate at the other end of it, that
something unusual was occurring in the
outer court of all, the Court of the Gentiles.
So I and some of the other younger members of the Sanhedrim passed rapidly
through the Court of the Women, and,
hurrying through the Beautiful Gate, found
Jesus preaching to the people under Solomon's Porch. Now, it is usual for the
people to make way when any member of
the Sanhedrim passes by ; but the people
were so engrossed with the words of Jesus

that they took no note of me and my companions, and we had to stand at the edge of the crowd and listen as best we might, and so great was the crowd that I could scarcely hear what the Nazarene was saying, until gradually those near us, recognizing the marks of our dignity, made way for us till we got nearer.

Never saw I Jesus in so exalted a state. Though he was not tall, as I have said, he seemed to tower above the crowd. The mid-day sun of winter was shining full upon the Temple, and though Jesus was in the shadow of the porch, the sunlight from the Temple walls shone back upon his eyes and hair, which gleamed with the glory of the sun. He looked and spake as a king among men. And, indeed, he was claiming to be something even greater than a king. I could not hear very distinctly from where I was at first, but towards the last, as I got nearer, I heard him say these words : —

" Whosoever committeth sin is the servant of sin. Except a man be born again, he cannot see the kingdom of God. He

that loveth his life shall lose it. If a man
keep my word he shall never see death,
but has passed from death unto life. He
that believeth in me, the works that I do
shall he do also. Yet can the Son do
nothing of himself, but what he seeth the
Father do. I am the door : by me, if any
man enter in, he shall be saved. I am the
Way, the Truth, and the Life. I am the
Light of the world. I am the good Shepherd, and know my sheep, and am known
of mine. I am the Bread of Life : he that
cometh to me shall never hunger. I am
the true Vine, and my Father is the Hus-
bandman. I am the Vine, ye are the
branches. If any man thirst, let him come
unto me and drink. Before Abraham was
I am."

Now, as Jesus was saying these words,
and many like unto them, his form seemed
to expand, his eye flashed with the light of
prophecy, and all men were amazed at the
power of his words. Never had they heard
man speak of himself with such confidence.
If he had been very God, he could not have
said more of his own power over men's

souls. Our prophets have spoken boldly
indeed, but none of them had boasted of
the power of the Lord in such terms as this
man spake of himself. Could he be mad,
I thought, to say such things? Yet in all
other matters he had shown a wisdom and
a sound sense equal to the greatest of our
Sages. Or had he found that by speaking
thus of himself, men, and above all, women,
were best moved to believe as he would
have them believe, to act as he would have
them act? Might it not be the simplest
of truths that for them, to them, he was
indeed the Way, the Truth, and the Life?

And, indeed, when I looked around and
saw the effect of his words on those who
were listening, I could in part understand
his power among men and women. They
drank in his words as travellers at the well
of the oasis. They lived upon his eyes,
and it was indeed strange to see every
man's body bent forward as of a straining
hound at the chase. If ever men worshipped a man, these were worshipping
Jesus.

And I? What was it with me that his
words failed to move me as they did those

around me? Why did his eyes rather re-
pel than attract me? Was it thy teaching, Aglaophonos, that had taught me the
way of thy race: to measure all things in
the balance of wisdom; to be moved in
all acts by reason, not feeling? Was it
from thee I learnt to think about the
causes of this man's influence, even while
I and others were under it? Perhaps not
alone; for much that this man was saying
would have repelled my Jewish instincts
even had I never come under thy influence. What struck thee among us Jews,
I remember, was that while we see the
Deity everywhere, we localize him no-
where. Alone among the nations of men
we refuse to make an image of our God.
We alone never regarded any man as God
Incarnate. Those among us who have
been nearest to the Divine have only
claimed to be — they have only been recognized to be — messengers of the Most
High. Yet here was this man, as it
seemed, claiming to be the Very God,
and all my Jewish feeling rose against the
claim.

Nor was I alone in this feeling I was

soon to learn.   Before Jesus had finished his harangue, cries arose from different quarters of the crowd.   " Blasphemy! " " Blasphemer! "   " He blasphemes! " arose on all sides.   These cries awakened men as if from a sleep, all turning round to see whence they came.   And the very turning round, as it were, removed them from the influence of Jesus and his eyes. In a moment, many of those who just before were hanging upon Jesus' words joined in the cry, " Blasphemer! blasphemer! "   One of the boldest of those who began the cry called out, " Blasphemer!   Stone him! "

But Jesus drew himself up, and looked upon the crowd with flashing eyes, and said, " O Jerusalem, Jerusalem! Sodom is justified of thee."   For a moment all were silent, but soon the cries arose again: " Blasphemer! blasphemer!   Stone him! "

Then began great commotion among the people.   While some called out, " Stone him! "   " Stone him! "   others cried, " Sacrilege! "   " Sacrilege! "   " No stoning in the Temple! "   And one called out with a jeer, " In the Temple ye cannot

stone, for lo! here there be no stones;"
and a bitter, scornful laugh followed his
words. Then some who were nearest to
Jesus sought to lay hands on him, while
others, his friends, stood round him and
prevented their approaching, and all was
confusion and tumult. When suddenly
the blare of a trumpet sounded through
the courts, and all cried, "The Romans!
the Romans!"

Then round by the royal porch came a
company of Roman soldiers to change the
sentries at mid-day, and they halted near
the Beautiful Gate. And as they came
near the crowd began to disperse, and
Jesus and his friends went their way from
the courts of the Temple.

That day, there was no talk in Jerusalem but of the event in the Temple. Men
marvelled at the way in which this Jesus
had spoken of himself. "The prophets
spake not thus," they said. "Yet how
can a man be greater than a prophet, who
speaketh the words of the Most High?
Even if we had once more a king over us
in Israel, he could not be as great as a
prophet, and no king would speak of him-

self as Jesus this day hath spoken of himself." But what if this man were destined
to be the Christ, the God-given Ruler that
should restore the throne of David? But
how could that be, since none of the signs
and portents of the last times had come
upon the earth? Who had seen the blood
trickle from the rocks? or the fiery sword
appear in the midnight sky? Had babes
a year old spoken like men? But others
said, " Nay, the kingdom of God will not
come with expectation. As it hath been
said, ' Three things come unexpectedly —
a scorpion, a treasure-trove, and the Messiah.'" And again, others said, "Perchance this is not the Messiah ben David,
but the Messiah ben Joseph, who shall be
slain before the other cometh." Thus the
minds of men and their words went hither
and thither about the sayings of this man
Jesus in the Temple.

X.

THE ENTRY INTO JERUSALEM.

X.

I HEARD naught and saw naught of Jesus
the Nazarene till the very last week of his
life, and that was the week before the Passover. The winter had been a severe one,
and much misery had arisen among the
folk through the exactions of the Romans;
indeed, an attempt had been made to throw
off the Roman yoke. In several places the
people had assembled in arms and attacked
the soldiery, and in some cases had slain
their sentries. Pilate had but sent off a
cohort into the district, and all signs of
discontent went underground. One of the
leaders of the revolt, Jesus Bar Abbas, had
been captured and thrown into prison.
He, indeed, had attempted an insurrection
in Jerusalem itself, where he was well
known and popular among the common
folk. When he was arrested, a riot had
occurred, and one of the soldiers was slain
who had been sent to arrest him; wherefore he lay now in prison on the charges of

rebellion and murder. Yet many thought
that this man had been put forth to try the
temper of the people and the power of the
Romans, in preparation for a more serious
attempt to shake off the oppressor.

Yet who should lead the people? Jochanan, the only man whom of recent times
the people followed gladly, had been done
to death by Herod. One man alone since
his death had won the people's heart, to
wit, Jesus the cousin of Jochanan. He,
and he alone, could lead the people against
the Romans, and all men wondered if he
would. In the midst of their wonder came
news that Jesus the Nazarene was coming
up to the Holy City for the Feast of Passover, the feast of redemption from Egypt.
Would it prove this year a feast of redemption from the Romans? All hope of this
depended upon this Jesus.

It was twenty-one years ago, but I can
remember as if it were yesterday the excitement in Jerusalem when the news came
that Jesus of Nazareth had arrived in the
neighborhood, and was spending his Sabbath at the village of Bethany. All those
who were disaffected against the Romans

cried out, "A leader! a leader!" All those
who were halt, sick, or blind, cried out, " A
healer! a healer!" Wherever we went,
there was no talk but of the coming deliverance. As I approached one group of
men I heard them say, " When will it be?
When will he give the sign? Will it be
before or after the feast?" "Nay," said
one of the crowd, a burly blacksmith he,
"what day for the deliverance but the
Passover day? But be it when it may, let
him give the sign, and I shall be ready."

" And prove a new Maccabee," said one
in the crowd, referring to his hammer,
whereat a grim laugh arose.

The next day being the first of the
week, which the Romans call the Day of
the Sun, I was pondering the words of the
Law in my little study chamber near the
roof of my father's house in the Street of
the Bakers near Herod's Palace, which at
that time was inhabited by the Procurator,
when suddenly I heard the patter of many
feet in the street beneath me, and looking
out, I saw them all hurrying, as it seemed,
to the Temple. I put on my sandals, and
taking my staff in my hand and drawing

my mantle over my head, hurried out after
the passers-by. But when they came to
the Broad Place before the Water Gate,
they turned sharp to the right, and went
down the Tyropœon as far as the Fountain
Gate, where I overtook them. There I
found all the most turbulent of the city
population. Some of the men I knew had
been engaged in the recent riot under
Jesus Bar Abbas. Others were the leading
Zealots in Jerusalem, and all were men
eager for the freeing of the city from the
Romans. And among them, too, were
others who cared not for freedom, nor
hated the Romans, but would only be too
pleased if the city were given up to disor-
der and rapine. While these waited there,
we heard cries from behind us, and looking
back, saw filing out from the Temple courts
on to the Xystus Bridge, and down into
the Tyropœon, the brigade of beggars who
pass almost their whole life in the Court of
the Gentiles. These came down slowly,
for among them were many halt and some
blind, and all were old and feeble of limb.
" Why come they forth from the courts ? "
I asked; " and why are we waiting? "

Then said one near me, " Knowest thou
not that Jesus the Nazarene enters the
city to-day? And men say he is to deliver
us." And at that moment a cry arose
among the folk, " Lo! there he is." Looking south, for a time I could see nothing,
for the mid-day sun of the spring solstice
was shining with that radiance which we
Jews think is only to be seen in our land.
But after a while I could discern, turning
the corner of the Jericho Road near En
Rogel, a mounted man, surrounded by a
number of men and women on foot. " It
is Jesus — it is Jesus!" all cried; "let us
to meet him!" And with that, all but the
lame rushed forward to meet him, and I
with them.

It is but three hundred paces from the
Fountain Gate to En Rogel, and the Nazarene and his friends had advanced somewhat to meet us, but in that short space
the enthusiasm of the crowd had arisen to
a very fever, and as we neared him one
cried out, and all joined in the cry, " Hosanna Barabba! Hosanna Barabba!" and
then they shouted our usual cry of welcome, " Blessed be he that cometh in the

name of the Lord!" and one bolder than
his fellows called out, "Blessed be the coming of the kingdom!" At that there was
the wildest joy among the people. Some
tore off branches of palms, and stood by
the way and waved them in front of Jesus;
others took off each his *talith* and threw it
down in front of the young ass on which
Jesus rode, as if to pave the way into the
Holy City with choice linen. But when I
looked upon the face of Jesus, there were
no signs there of the coming triumph; he
sat with his head bent forward, his eyes
downcast, and his face all sad. And a
chill somehow came over me. I thought
of that play of the Greeks which thou
gavest me to read, in which the king of
men, driving to his own palace at Argos,
is enticed to enter it, stepping upon soft
carpets like an idol of your gods, and so
incurs the divine jealousy.

As we approached the Fountain Gate,
the beggars from the Temple had come
down to it, and joined in the shouting
and the welcome; and one of them,
Tobias ben Pinchas by name, who had,
ever since men had known him, walked

with a crutch, suddenly, in his excitement, raised his crutch and waved it over his head, and danced before Jesus, crying, " Hosanna Barabba! Hosanna Barabba!" and all men cried out, " A miracle, a miracle! what cannot this man perform?" And so, with a crowd surrounding him, Jesus entered Jerusalem and went up into the Temple. But I that year had been appointed one of the overseers who distributed the unleavened bread to the poor of the city for the coming Passover, and I had then to attend the meeting of my fellow-overseers.

That night there was no talk in Jerusalem but of the triumphant entry of Jesus. The city was crowded by Israelites who had come up to the capital for the festival, and a whisper went about that many of the strangers had been summoned by Jesus to Jerusalem to help in the coming revolt. During that night, wherever a Roman sentry stood, a crowd of the unruly would collect round him and jeer at him; and in one place the sentry had to use his spear, and wounded one of the crowd. So great was the tumult that,

when the sentries were changed for the
midnight watch, a whole company of soldiers accompanied the officer's guard and
helped to clear the streets. Meanwhile,
where was Jesus? And what was he
doing in the midst of this tumult? I
made inquiry, for perchance he might
have been holding disputations about the
Law, as is the custom with our Sages; but
I learnt that he had left the city at the
eleventh hour, and gone back to the village of Bethany, where he was staying.
But I was thinking through all that evening of the strange contrast between the
triumphant joy of his followers and the
saddened countenance of the Nazarene.

Men knew not what was to become of
this movement in favor of him. Most of
the lower orders were hoping for a rising
against the Romans to be led by this Jesus. Shrewder ones among the Better
thought that the man was about to initiate
a change in the spiritual government of
our people. Some thought he would de-
pose the Sadducees, and place the Pharisees in their stead. Others feared that
he would carry into practice the ideals

of the *Ebionim*, and raise the Poor against the Rich. Others said, " Why did he not enter by the gate of the Essenes, for he holdeth with them ? " All knew that the coming Passover would be a trying time for Israel, owing to the presence of the man Jesus in Jerusalem, and the manifest favor in which he was held by the common folk. But amidst all this I could see only the pale, sad face of Jesus.

XI.

THE CLEANSING OF THE TEMPLE

XI.

On the morrow, being the second day
of the week, which the Romans call the
Day of the Moon, Jesus of Nazara came
early into Jerusalem, and as soon as it was
known that he had entered the city, all
those that had gone out to greet him on
the previous day, and many more with
them who had heard of the miracle that
he had performed, went to meet him in
the Broad Place. And near upon the
time of the mid-day sacrifice, Jesus and all
these men went up to the Temple.

Now, I have told thee how, when Jesus
had first come to Jerusalem, he had driven
forth from the Court of the Gentiles all
those who were engaged in selling beasts
of sacrifice, or in changing foreign moneys
for the shekels. But the money-changers
and others had been replaced by the
orders of the High Priest Hanan, and
nothing had come of this action, nor in
his later visits to Jerusalem had he done

aught in the matter, and it was thought
that he had acknowledged the right and
the power of the priests to have the monopoly of the sale of sacrifices. Now,
that day of the Moon was the tenth day of
the month Nisan, and upon it were purchased all the lambs for the forthcoming
Passover sacrifices, as it is said in the
Law, " In the tenth day of this month
they shall take to them every man a lamb
according to the house of their fathers,
a lamb for an house." As this Paschal
sacrifice is the only home sacrifice of us
Jews, thou mightest imagine that each
householder could obtain his lamb whence
he would ; but the priests say " No " to
this, for if a man could take any chance
lamb, it might not be without blemish.
So it had grown to be a custom that, on
the morning of the tenth day of Nisan,
the heads of households in Jerusalem
should wend their way to the courts of
the Temple, there to select each man a
lamb. And the priests had their profit
in this, for they claimed from those who
sold the lambs dues for every animal allowed to be in the courts. And the sellers

again were agreeable to this, for none that had not the favor could sell the Paschal lambs. Whence it was that the price of a lamb in the Paschal week was more than three times as much as at any time of the year, and the poorer people murmured greatly.

Thus it happened that upon this day, when Jesus came into the courts of the Temple, these were crowded with all the householders of Jerusalem, and much chaffering and haggling was going on in the purchase of the lambs for the Passover. But Jesus, with the favor he had won from the people, was for this day at least Ruler of Jerusalem, and men wondered what he would do with regard to this sale and purchase of the beasts of sacrifice; for on his first coming to Jerusalem, as I have told thee, he had driven the sellers away, but afterwards, when they had been restored to their places, he had seemed to acquiesce. What would he do now, men thought, as they saw him advancing over the Xystus Bridge, the head of a vast concourse of people who would do all that he told them?

They had not long to wait, for no sooner had he entered the Temple courts, than he spake to those around him, and ordered them to remove the tables of the money-changers, with their weights and scales, without which no purchase could be; and no man dared say him nay, for all knew that the people were with him. And they, indeed, were rejoiced, for they took this as permission to buy their Paschal lambs where they would; and many of those who had been bargaining in the courts of the Temple went off at once to the market, and got them their lambs from thence. All this I heard of in the inner courts of the Temple, for it chanced that day that I had to offer a sin offering, and was waiting my turn in the Court of the Israelites while the priests were preparing the mid-day sacrifice. And I saw one coming up to Hanan and to Joseph Caiaphas, who were presiding over the sacrifice, and they spake earnestly to one another, and stopped the sacrifice, and came through the Court of the Israelites and went down the Court of the Women, and all of us followed them thither. And when we came to the Beautiful Gate, and turned to the right round the corner of the Temple, behold, we saw the flocks of Paschal lambs being driven through the Western Gates. And in the midst of the court stood Jesus, surrounded by a multitude clamoring and shouting. Then saw I Hanan lean over to Joseph Caiaphas, his son-in-law, and speak somewhat to him. Then the latter advanced in front of the priests and the scribes, who had come forth with him, and asked, " Who hath done this? " And Jesus said, " It is I." Then spake Joseph again and said, " Tell us, by what authority doest thou these things? And who gave thee this authority? "

Now, Joseph the High Priest was clad this day in the robes of his office, with tiara on head, the ephod on his breast, and silver bells and pomegranates round the edge of his garment. Whereas Jesus the Nazarene wore his wonted garb of a common country workman. Yet for the moment this common workman was the greater power of the two; since all men knew how he had been received by the

people when he had come into Jerusalem,
and that what he willed, all the people of
Jerusalem willed also at that time. So all
were hushed to hear what this Jesus would
say to the question of the High Priest,
since now they thought he must declare
himself, and justify the power he was exer-
cising.

But here again, as on former occasions,
Jesus answered not directly to the question
of the priests, but rather questioned them.
He said, " I also ask you one thing, which
if ye tell me, I likewise will tell you by
what authority I do these things. The
baptism of Jochanan, was it from heaven
or of men ? Answer me." And they answered and said unto Jesus, " We cannot
tell." Then said Jesus unto them, " Then
neither will I tell by what authority I do
these things. To what is the matter like ?
There was a man had two sons. And the
man came to the first, and said, ' My son,
go work in my vineyard.' But he said, ' I
will not.' Howbeit afterward he repented,
and went to work. But the man went to
the second, and spake in like manner. But
he answered, ' I go, sir.' But yet he went

not. Whether of these twain did the will
of his father?" And we all answered,
"The first." Then Jesus looked slowly
around at us all, and said, "This I say
unto you, the publicans and harlots enter
into the kingdom of heaven before you.
For Jochanan came unto you in the way
of righteousness, and ye heeded him not,
but the harlots and the publicans heeded
him : but ye, even when ye saw this, repented not."

Now, at this public insult to all of
priestly rank, I saw dart forward Hanan
the High Priest, as if he would have rent
the man Jesus. But Caiaphas his son-in-
law caught him by the wrist, and whispered
words in his ear. But Hanan broke
loose, and called out in a loud voice, "My
guard, my guard!" Whereat many of the
folk who had come with Jesus into the
Court of the Gentiles came forward round
him, and put their hands to their weapons. He indeed said naught, nor seemed
aware of the conflict that threatened.
But Caiaphas turned, and in a loud voice
said, "I go to perform the mid-day sacrifice," and walked slowly out of the court

back to the Temple. And we all followed
him.

Now, when we returned from perform-
ing the sacrifice, Jesus had left the courts
of the Temple, which had become bare
and empty of people. And as I went
homeward to my house in the Street of
the Bakers, I looked down from the
Xystus Bridge, and saw trooping down
the Tyropœon Jesus and a great multitude
of the people, who crowded round him,
as if eager to touch the hem of his garment. I stood and watched till they
reached the Fountain Gate, through which
he passed; and shortly afterwards I could
see him on the road to the Fountain of
Rogel, still accompanied by many of the
people.

What was to come of that day's work I
knew not. For the first time the discontent of the common folk with the man-
agement of the Temple by the priests
had come to a head, and had resulted in
this open conflict between Jesus and the
High Priests. The city was full of strangers excited by thoughts of the coming
festival. The common people had not yet

calmed themselves from the thoughts of rebellion which had been raised by the rising of Jesus Bar Abbas and others. The
whole city was as tow ready for the spark
of fire.

XII.

THE WOES.

XII.

Now, on the morrow, being the third
day of the week, Jesus of Nazara came
again into the city, and the rumor of his
coming spread through all the streets and
places of Jerusalem. And going forth
after the morning prayers, I found Jesus
with many around him in the Broad Place
before the Water Gate. And as I approached near to them, I saw the crowd
part asunder and a procession coming
through, and almost all the men there
bowed and did reverence to the men who
were passing through. Now, these were
mostly of the Pharisaic sect, who were
going to the Great Beth Hamidrash, to
pursue the study of the Law and to give
decisions on legal questions which the
common folk put to them. And at their
head walked Jochanan ben Zaccai, the President of the Tribunal. He was regarded
as the most capable exponent of the Law
since the death of Hillel, whose favorite

pupil he had been, and men were wont to
refer to him for decision in all the most
difficult questions of life. He was walking
at the head of the procession in his long
talith with large borders and in his broad
phylacteries. And he passed Jesus with a
salutation, indeed, but in it was mingled
some of the pride and contempt with which
the masters of the Law regarded all those
whom they call the Country-folk.

When these had passed, Jesus turned
round to the people, and spake these words:

"The scribes and the Pharisees sit in
Moses' seat : all therefore whatsoever they
bid you observe, that observe and do ; but
do not ye after their works : for they say,
and do not. For they bind heavy burdens
and grievous to be borne, and lay them on
men's shoulders ; but they themselves will
not move them with one of their fingers.
But all their works they do for to be seen
of men : they make broad their phylacteries, and enlarge the borders of their garments, and love the chief place at feasts,
and the chief seats in the synagogues, and
greetings in the markets, and to be called
of men, ' Rabbi, Rabbi.'

" But be not ye called Rabbi : for One is your Master, and all ye are brethren.

"And call no man your father upon the earth : for One is your Father, which is in heaven.

" Neither be ye called Masters, for One is your Master.

" But he that is greatest among you shall be your servant. And whosoever shall exalt himself shall be abased; and he that shall humble himself shall be exalted.

" But woe unto you, scribes and Pharisees, hypocrites ! for ye shut up the kingdom of heaven against men : for ye neither go in yourselves, neither suffer ye them that are entering to go in.

" Woe unto you, scribes and Pharisees, hypocrites ! for ye devour widows' houses, and for a pretence make long prayers : therefore ye shall receive the greater damnation.

" Woe unto you, scribes and Pharisees, hypocrites ! for ye compass sea and land to make one proselyte, and when he is made, ye make him twofold more the child of hell than yourselves.

" Woe unto you, blind guides, which say,

' Whosoever shall swear by the Temple, it
is nothing ; but whosoever shall swear
by the gold of the Temple, he is bound ! '
Ye fools and blind ! for whether is greater,
the gold, or the Temple that sanctifieth
the gold ?   And, ' Whosoever shall swear
by the altar, it is nothing ; but whosoever
sweareth by the gift that is upon it, he is
bound ! '   Ye fools and blind ! for whether
is greater, the gift, or the altar that sanctifieth the gift ?   Whoso, therefore, shall
swear by the altar, sweareth by it, and by
all things thereon.   And whoso shall swear
by the Temple, sweareth by it, and by him
that dwelleth therein.   And he that shall
swear by heaven, sweareth by the throne
of God, and by him that sitteth thereon.

" Woe unto you, scribes and Pharisees,
hypocrites ! for ye pay tithe of mint and
anise and cummin, and have omitted the
weightier matters of the Law, judgment,
mercy, and faith ; these ought ye to have
done, and not to leave the other undone.

" Ye blind guides, which strain out the
gnat and swallow a camel !

" Woe unto you, scribes and Pharisees,
hypocrites ! for ye make clean the outside

of the cup and of the platter, but within they are full of extortion and excess. Thou blind Pharisee! cleanse first that which is within the cup and platter, that the outside of them may be clean also.

"Woe unto you, scribes and Pharisees, hypocrites! for ye are like unto whited sepulchres, which indeed appear beautiful outward, but are within full of dead men's bones, and of all uncleanness. Even so ye also outwardly appear righteous unto men, but within ye are full of hypocrisy and iniquity.

"Woe unto you, scribes and Pharisees, hypocrites! because ye build the tombs of the prophets, and garnish the sepulchres of the righteous, and say, 'If we had been in the days of our fathers, we would not have been partakers with them in the blood of the prophets.' Fill ye up, then, the measure of your fathers. Ye serpents, ye generation of vipers, how can ye escape the damnation of hell?"

And all the people were astonished at these words, for in many of his sayings and most of his actions Jesus had seemed to

incline more to the sect of the Pharisees
than to any other section of the house of
Israel. And, indeed, in the opening words
of his discourse he had granted their right
to interpret the Law and to lead the people.
Yet wherefore had he denounced them all
without distinction as men insincere and
void of truth? Hypocrites there were
among them as among other classes of
men. Often, indeed, their acts did not go
with their words; but of what man can
it be said that all his acts and words go
together? These men were occupied in
building a rampart to the Law, and holding the fortress against enemies without
and dissensions within. Those ramparts
might confine our actions within a narrow
space, yet is it not well for all men to be
kept perforce in the path of duty? I know
thou thinkest otherwise, Aglaophonos.
Thy Master the Stagyrite has taught thee
that man should be a law unto himself;
but we Jews willingly bear the yoke of the
Law, because we believe it to be the yoke
of the Lord. And in this matter Jesus
had in every way shown himself to be a
Jew of the Jews. Why, then, was he so

in wrath against the interpreters of the
Law?

Yet were the common folk not displeased
at these sayings of Jesus; nay, rather they
applauded them. For in many ways our
Sages have failed to find favor with the
common folk of Israel; for besides that
they would regulate their lives at every
point, so that no man dare do this or do
that except in the way the Sages prescribe,
but chiefly the rabbis were out of favor with
the folk for that they did openly despise
and condemn all but those who were learned
in the Law. The unlearned they called the
Country-folk. Wherefore did the people
hear with pleasure the bitter words Jesus
spake against the scribes and the Pharisees.

The night of that same day an event
occurred which roused the city of Jerusalem to a pitch of expectation such as I had
never seen there. Two young Zealots,
artisans, that were popular with their fellows for their kindness of heart and good
humor, fell into an altercation with a Roman officer near the Sheep Gate, not far
from Antonia, where all the Roman soldiers
lie. Without a word of warning, the Ro-

man officer drew his sword and killed one
of these young men, and when his compan-
ion and the passers-by rebuked him, and
would have seized him to take him before
the procurator, he gave a signal, and a
multitude of soldiers poured forth from
Antonia and struck without mercy among
the crowd. Five were killed and many
were wounded, and the whole city was in
an uproar at this proof of Roman insolence. " How long, O Lord? " the gray-
beards said, raising their hands to heaven.
And the younger men said, " Let us but
wait the coming of Jesus the Liberator;
surely before the Passover he will free us
from the rule of the *Goyim.*"

XIII.

THE GREAT REFUSAL.

XIII.

Thou canst imagine with what feelings of expectation all Jerusalem awaited the coming of Jesus next morning. Many of the Pharisees had come together the eve before, and spoken of the public insult Jesus had given to their sect on the preceding day. Hanan the High Priest, we heard, had quarrelled furiously with his son-in-law Joseph Caiaphas, for that he had not allowed him to summon his guard after the humiliation he had put upon them in the Temple. Yet neither the Pharisees nor the Sadducees who followed the High Priests dared lay hands upon this Jesus, because of the evident favor in which he was held by the common folk of Jerusalem, and above all by the many from country parts who had come up, like him, to spend the Passover in the Holy City. Among all these there was no talk but of Jesus the Liberator; nay! many spake of him as Jesus the

Christ. And if he were indeed to be the Christ, the King of Israel, the Founder of the New Kingdom, it could not be that he would suffer longer the yoke of the Romans to lie upon the neck of Israel.

Yet there was one thing that perplexed many, and opinion went hither and thither among the minds of men concerning it. The Christ who was to deliver Israel and to rule over mankind, was he not to be the son of David? Yet this Jesus was of Galilee, where the admixture of blood had been greatest in all Israel. " There is no unleavened bread in all Galilee," the scoffers used to say, meaning thereby that their genealogy was sprinkled with yeast, as we call foreign admixture. And for this man's genealogy, who could declare it? Many, indeed, as I have told thee, thought him to have no right even to be called son of his father. A *mamzer* shall not sit in the congregation of Israel. How, then, could one ascend Israel's throne?

When, therefore, Jesus came next morning from his lodging in Bethany, all Jerusalem turned out to welcome him, for the

Passover was coming anear, and if aught
was to be done to clear the city of the
Romans, it must be done quickly, must be
done on that day. Never saw I the courts
of the Temple so crowded as on that day
when I came thither, and found Jesus
standing in the Court of the Gentiles,
with almost all the leading men of Jerusalem and many of the common folk surg-
ing about him. Scarce room was left for
the Roman sentry to march his guard in
front of the Beautiful Gate. Yet he took
no heed of us barbarians, but with shield
and spear shouldered his way backward
and forward, backward and forward, a
sign to all men that the house of God
was in the hands of God's enemies.

Never saw I the men of Jerusalem so
exultant as on that morning. Wherever
I looked, joy — a grim joy — was on every
man's countenance, and there was no man
there but was armed, save only Jesus himself and some ten or a dozen men who had
come with him from Bethany, and these,
indeed, were the only men who had not
shown joy. Never had I seen the Nazarene with a countenance so saddened and

aweary. Yestermorn he had been flashing
with anger and indignation as he spake
his words against the Pharisees, but on
this day his force seemed to be spent, and
he appeared like one who had passed
through a great agony.

Now, as they were standing there, I saw
a man, one of the leaders of the Zealots,
armed as if for battle, go up and lay a
hand upon one of those with Jesus. He
spake eagerly with him, and pointed with
his thumb to the Roman soldier as he
passed to and fro. But the other shook
his head vehemently, and took his arm
away from the grasp of the Zealot and
turned his back upon him.

Now, at this moment certain of the
Pharisees came through the crowd and
advanced to Jesus. So great was the
crowd that I heard not at first what they
said unto him; but it must have been
some question about the matter that was
in all men's minds, for I heard his reply,
and that, as was his wont, was in the form
of a counter-question to their inquiry, for
he said, "What think *ye* of the Christ?
Whose son is he?" And they, speaking

with the thought of all Israel, said, " The Christ is the son of David."

Then all men watched with expectancy to hear what the Nazarene would say to this; for if he agreed with them, then would he deny himself to be the Christ: for his genealogy had by no means been proven. But yet, how could he disprove the belief of all Israel, that the Christ was the Son of David? Yet that did he after the manner of our Sages, using words of Scripture as his confirmation; for he said unto them, " How then is it that David himself saith in the Book of Psalms, ' The Lord said unto my Lord, Sit thou on my right hand until I make thine enemies thy footstool'? David therefore himself calleth the Christ Lord; how then can the Christ be his son?"

At this the Pharisees knew not what to say, for no man had hitherto used that *stichos* of the Psalms, and they knew not what to reply. But the common folk were rejoiced exceedingly; joy spread on their faces, and I saw many a fist raised and shaken in exultant defiance at the Roman sentry, who walked hither and thither on his guard as if he were a living mass of steel.

Thereupon certain of the crowd who were known to be followers of Herod had speech with Jesus, and spake to him: " Master, we know that thou art true, and carest for no man; that thou regardest not the person of men, but teachest the way of God in all truth — tell us, therefore, what thinkest thou: is it lawful to give tribute to Cæsar or not? shall we give, or shall we not give?" All men were silent, and drew their breath to hear what Jesus might say to this. For if he claimed to be the Anointed One, to whom but to the King of Israel should Israel's tribute be paid?

But he said unto them, " Why tempt ye me? Bring me a denarius, that I may see it." And they brought one and put it into his hand. And he held it forth unto them, and said, " Whose is this image and superscription?" And they answered, " Cæsar's." And then Jesus said unto them, " Render to Cæsar the things that are Cæsar's, and to God the things that are God's." And these Herodians mar-

velled at the subtlety with which he had
answered them, but the common folk were
amazed and dumfounded at his answer.
And soon I heard one say to another, " He
denieth: he would pay tribute to Cæsar."
And gradually all the men drew away from
him, leaving him alone with only the company with him from Bethany.

But he, seeing this, turned to one of
those with him, and said, " Peter, of whom
do the kings of the earth take custom?
of their own children, or of the aliens?"
And Peter answered and said, " Of the
aliens." Then Jesus said to him, " Then
are the children free?" And Peter said
to him, " Yes." Then said Jesus unto him,
" Then do thou also give, as being an alien
to them." The common folk heard this,
indeed, but were in no wise satisfied. If
they were to give tribute to the Romans
for whatever cause, they were still to be
under subjection to Rome, and then Jesus
refused to be their Liberator; that had
become clear to them of a sudden. And
they drew still further away from him.
And a deep silence of mortification fell
upon all men there, so that thou couldst

hear distinctly the tread of the Roman sentry as he moved on his march.

Amid the deep silence suddenly came a gentle tinkling, as of silver bells; it came nearer and nearer, and a crier called out, "Way for the High Priests!" Then Hanan the High Priest, with Caiaphas his son-in-law, and others of the priests accompanied by their guard, came down the steps from the Beautiful Gate. The Roman sentry stopped his march and stood upright, with spear on ground, and all made way as the procession of the High Priests passed through the court. All men were silent, and thou couldst hear the tinkling of the silver bells which were attached to the hems of the High Priests' garments. Hanan walked at the head of the procession with his usual haughty gait, and had nearly passed through the court, when he saw Jesus and those with him. At once he halted, and summoned one of the crowd to him. Then we saw much eager talk between this man and the High Priest. And Hanan summoned the captain of his guard, who would have turned towards Jesus, but that Joseph

Caiaphas stayed him and spake unto Hanan, pointing to the Roman sentry. After much talk between these, the High Priests resumed their march and left the Temple. And all the other men began to pass away from the court, leaving Jesus and his men alone with none to listen to him. For the word passed swiftly in the mouths of all the men of Jerusalem, — " He refuseth; he would have us be slaves of the Romans forever."

XIV.

THE MEETING OF THE HANANITES.

XIV.

THE next day being the fifth day of the week, and the thirteenth day of the month Nisan in that year, many rumors went about the city as to the man Jesus. There were who said that he had been seized by the guards of Hanan; others said that he had left the village of Bethany and gone no man knew whither. But for that day Jesus came not into Jerusalem, and men's minds were occupied more with one of the difficulties of our Law which form the occupation and delight of our Sages. I must explain this unto thee, for upon it turn the events of the next day, so fateful for the man about whom thou art inquiring. Thou canst easily understand what I shall say, for thou hast, I know, a copy of the Scriptures in Greek, for did I not procure it for thee?

It is said in the Law, thou wilt find, that the Passover lamb is to be killed in the twilight between the fourteenth and the

fifteenth of Nisan, and it is also said in our
Law that the whole of the lamb must be
consumed that evening. Now, in the
years when the fifteenth of Nisan, which
is the first day of the Passover, falleth
upon the Sabbath, the killing and roasting
of the lamb would take place on the Sabbath eve, when no killing must take place
and no fire must be lit. Hence arises a
conflict of the Law of the Passover with
the Law of the Sabbath. Now, the older
view was, that the Passover was superior
to the Sabbath, and its law was to be followed in preference. This the priests
held and followed, and in this they seemed
to have the authority of the great Hillel,
who also declared the Passover superior to
the Sabbath.

But many among the Pharisees and the
more pious preferred to slay the Passover
lamb on the eve between the thirteenth
and the fourteenth day of Nisan, and to
eat it on the fourteenth day; that is, in
those years when the Passover fell on the
Sabbath, as was the case in the year of
which I am now writing. It would appear
that Jesus and his followers held with the

latter opinion, for, as I have heard, on the eve of the fourteenth of Nisan he came stealthily into the city of Jerusalem, and ate the Passover lamb concealed in an upper chamber of one of his friends in the city. It showeth how earnest this man was in following the larger precepts of the Law, though in smaller matters he seemed to neglect it. For by this time he must have known that he was no longer safe in Jerusalem ; and, indeed, he proved this by his secret entry into it. Yet in order to fulfil the Law, which saith, " The Passover lamb is to be eaten in Jerusalem," he risked his own and his followers' lives. Yet was he careful of them; for, as thou shalt soon hear, as soon as he had gone through the meal prescribed by the Law, he escaped out of Jerusalem.

Now, that night I was standing at the door of my house, looking upon the city bathed in the light of the moon, which was near its full, when suddenly a man seized me by the arm and said, " Thou art wanted." I looked, and behold it was Simon Kantheros, my brother-in-law. And I said to him, " Who wants me ? and wherefore?" And Simon answered me and said, " Hanan the High Priest has summoned suddenly a meeting of the Sanhedrim at his house on the Mount of Olives." Then said I, " But if it be at his house, it can only be the Priestly Sanhedrim of Twenty-Three that he summons." "Nay, nay, man," answered Simon, " the case is urgent. He saith, ' any member of the Sanhedrim.' Come, then, with me, and quickly." So with that I seized my mantle and my staff, and went forth with him.

So we hurried across the market-place towards the Fish Gate, and as we passed near the Tower Antonia, we saw the flashing of red lights, and heard hoarse cries of command, and knew not what was toward. But when we arrived at the Fish Gate, we found them changing the sentries of the first watch, and knew that the second watch had begun. At first the sentry would not let us through the gate; but the officer was called, and Simon showed him his badge as member of the Sanhedrim. But even this would not have sufficed, but that Simon then pointed to his toga and the purple stripe, which showed that he was a Roman citizen of rank. Thereat the officer spake to the sentry, and we passed through the gate, and turned sharply to the right, and went down the road which leads to the valley of the Kidron. And as we were passing the Brook Kidron, we looked and saw dots of red light moving up the hill from the Garden of Gethsemane. And as we advanced up the hill of the Mount of Olives, we could see from time to time these red sparks preceding us; and when we came within sight of the High Priest's house, we saw them enter in and disappear.

Soon we ourselves had come up to the gate, and when we knocked, a wicket was opened, and a face peered out, and our names were asked. When we had told them, the gate was closed, and we had to wait some time. But at last the door was opened, and the captain of the guard received us. He took us through the passage which led into the open court, with the water-basin in the centre, round which we skirted, and ascended the steps into the inner house. And again we stopped before the hall-door while our names were asked, and again we had to wait till the door was at last opened. Then at last we entered the hall, and found Joseph Caiaphas the High Priest and many of his kinsmen seated round a long table. Caiaphas rose, and motioned us to two seats at the end of this table, and we seated ourselves.

When my eyes had become accustomed to the light, I looked round, and said the greeting of peace unto those I knew of the assembly. I can still remember many of their names. There was Ishmael ben Phabi, who had at first replaced Hanan as High Priest. There were also the four sons of Hanan — Eleazar, Jonathan, Theophilus, and Matthias. Then there were Kamithos the priest, and his two sons, Simon and Joseph. And beside these, I remember two men of my own generation — Elioni ben Kantheros and Chananyah ben Nedebai. Most of these men had been, or were afterwards, High Priests, and were all at this time members of the Priestly Sanhedrim. On the left of Caiaphas was a low stool, and, even as I looked,

Hanan ben Seth the High Priest came in swiftly from a side door, and took a seat thereon. He glanced sharply round at each of us, counting our numbers, and we were exactly three and twenty. And when he saw me, he rose and spake somewhat harshly, " Meshullam ben Zadok, what dost thou here? This is a meeting of the Priestly Sanhedrim. Thou art a son of Israel." And I answered and said, " Simon Kantheros here, my kinsman, summoned me to the meeting, saying that any member of the Sanhedrim could attend." The High Priest thought for a moment — he seemed as if he were counting us again — then he said, " Be it so ; thou art at least a true son of Israel, and this is not a formal meeting of the priests." He sat him down again, and we waited. At last an attendant entered by the same door, and, going up to the High Priest, spake to him. He nodded quickly, and dismissed him with a wave of his hand. And when he had passed through the door, Hanan the High Priest rose, and spake to us these words : —

" Kinsmen and colleagues, ye have all

heard, if ye have not witnessed, how Jesus
of Nazara entered the Holy City on the
first day of this week, amid the acclamations of his followers and many of the
lower people, who even went so far as to
hail him as the Deliverer. Now, to-morrow, as ye know, is the Passover. Who
knows, if the thoughts of deliverance from
Egypt, which come at that time, may not
cause this man, or, if not him, his followers,
to attempt a rising against the Romans our
masters? We know that any such attempt
would be entirely futile, but the very attempt itself would be the ruin of the nation.
Ye know the character of the man Pontius
Pilate. 'T is but a short time since he slew,
of wanton cruelty, certain Galilæans, even
while they were making sacrifices, and all
for mere suspicion of disaffection. Ye cannot but remember the building of Solomon's Aqueduct. Because money was
taken from the Temple treasury for the
building thereof, the people were inflamed,
and would have risen against them. What
did he but send his soldiers, disguised in
civil garb and armed with clubs, among the
people, when they came to make their pro-

test? And without warning, and in mere
wanton cruelty, did he give the signal for
massacre. If he did this at a mere threat
of a rising, what will happen should an
actual rising take place to-morrow? It is
our duty to see that such a calamity fall
not upon this nation because of the presence of this rude provincial in our midst.
Better one man should die than the nation
should suffer. No time was to be lost,
and I therefore have had this Jesus arrested, and he now awaits our pleasure in
the atrium.

"Before I summon him to our presence,
I would briefly state to you what seems to
me and some of our friends here the right
course to be followed. We purpose to
hand him over at dawn to Pontius Pilate,
to deal with him as he will. For he, by
his spies, and by the demonstration on the
first day of the week, must be aware of
the danger of a rising to-morrow night,
caused by this man's presence in our city.
Indeed, it is for the very purpose of pre-
venting a rising that he cometh up each
year about the Passover to Jerusalem.
Let it, then, be his care to prevent it how

he will; we shall have done our part, and he cannot punish the nation, or us its leaders.

" But some of you will say, Why should we deliver this man up to the Romans, perhaps, or even probably, to his death? I say, that even apart from the danger which he offers to the State, he is worthy of death for his manifest blasphemies. He speaketh of himself as very God, and claims to be the Anointed One, and puts aside the Law as it pleaseth him. I say naught of his insolence in the Temple cloisters, for this matter concerns us that be priests, and in the matter of judgment we must not take account of aught that deals with our private concerns; yet it is manifest that he hath no reverence for the Lord's house: witnesses shall prove to you that he hath said he would sweep it away and build another. I wonder not that horror is expressed in your faces at this blasphemy.

" Yet, as ye know, our Law hath in mercy provided that none shall be condemned unless on the testimony of witnesses. The Law shall be fulfilled. Even

now, as I speak, one of his followers,
Judas, a man of Kerioth, is drawing forth
from him his blasphemies before two witnesses, concealed, as is the custom. And
even if he fail, I know this man Jesus; in
his arrogance he will not scruple to repeat
his blasphemies, even before us.

"Time presses, and I have but this to
add before the prisoner is summoned: it
is a wise provision of our Law, that in
capital charges no final condemnation
shall occur until the second day of the
trial. The day before the Passover began
this eve. If we keep to the Law, no condemnation can take place till after the
first day of the Passover, by which time
all the mischance may have come to pass.
If the power of life and death were solely
in our hands, I would not depart in aught
from the wise provision of our forefathers;
but, in truth, if this man be put to death,
it will not be our doing, for his fate rests
with Pilate. I would remind the younger
members of the Sanhedrim that the final
decision is not with us, and if they vote
for this man's death, as I cannot doubt
they will, considering the pressing danger

to our nation, they need not fear to be
called members of a bloodthirsty Sanhedrim, since his death, if death he suffers,
will be at the hands of the Roman Procurator.   In this strait I propose, therefore,
to examine this man at once, and if, as I
doubt not, he avows his guilt, to wait till
the morning for his final condemnation,
and in this way fulfil the Law.   Summon
the prisoner to our presence."   Then,
turning to Caiaphas, he said, "This is a
matter between us and the Romans, for
whom thou, Joseph, art the High Priest.
Take thou, then, the interrogatory."

XV.

THE EXAMINATION BEFORE THE SANHEDRIM.

XV.

THEN from the lower end of the hall
entered Jesus the Nazarene, with his arms
bound with withes behind his back, and
he was led by the captain of the guard up
to the centre of the table opposite Caiaphas the High Priest. Then Caiaphas
rose, and, looking at a paper in his hand
which Hanan had given him, said unto
Jesus, "Jesus of Nazara, thou art accused
before us of blasphemy, and of leading the
people of Israel astray: what sayest thou
thereto?" Jesus gazed haughtily at him,
and answered, "I spake openly to all the
world, I have taught in the synagogue and
in the Temple, and in secret I have said
nothing. Why askest thou me? Ask
them which heard me what I have said
unto them. Behold, they know what I
have said." Then one of the men who
had led Jesus in struck him with the
palm of his hand, and said, "Answerest
thou the High Priest so?" But Jesus

turned, and said to him in a milder voice, " If I have said aught that is evil, bear witness thereof; but if well, why smitest thou me?" And Caiaphas the High Priest bade the man begone and bring in the witnesses. Then one man came forward and said he had heard Jesus call himself the Son of God. And another, that he had spoken of himself as if he were very God, and could do all that the Holy One, blessed be He, can perform. And yet another came forward and said he had heard Jesus speak of himself as Son of Man, and had thereby, as he thought, claimed to do what the Son of Man is said to do in the Prophets Daniel and Enoch. But no two of these witnesses agreed as to time and seasons, as is required by our Law. At last, however, two of them declared that on the preceding day in the Temple they had heard him say, " I will destroy this Temple that is made with hands, and in three days I will build another without hands." Now, during all this time Jesus had said naught, but looked before him with that rapt expression that I had seen upon him on the

second occasion when I had heard him
preach in the synagogue of the Galilæans.
So Caiaphas the High Priest spake to
him, saying, "Answerest thou naught to
what these men witness against thee?"
And Jesus made as if he heard not.

Then Hanan the High Priest leaned
over to Caiaphas his son-in-law and spake
some words to him. Then Caiaphas, rising, spake thus to Jesus: "Art thou the
Christ, the Son of the Holy One, blessed
be He?" Then Jesus raised his head,
and gazing fixedly at the High Priest,
said in a loud voice, "Thou hast said.
And hereafter ye shall see the Son of
Man sitting on the right hand of power,
and coming on the clouds of heaven."
Then Hanan the High Priest rose and
rent his clothes, as is our wont in time
of mourning or when blasphemy is heard,
and he called out in his keen, shrill voice,
"What need we any further witnesses?
Ye have heard the blasphemy; what think
ye?" And he waved his hand to the
captain of the guard, who removed the
prisoner.

When the door was closed behind him,

Hanan said, " What need we of further words? let us proceed to the judgment." And glancing over to Chananyah ben Nedebai, he said, " Chananyah, thou art the youngest; it is thine to pronounce judgment first. Is not this man guilty of death for his manifest blasphemy here before us?" And Chananyah said, " Yea." And so said all till Hanan had called upon thirteen to give judgment. Then said Hanan, " This man is for certain condemned to death, or at least to be handed over to the Roman Procurator: for already a majority of two have declared his death, even if all the rest were for an acquittal, as I cannot think possible. The Court will rise and reassemble at the time of the saying of the morning prayer, in order to confirm this judgment. Ye will not have long to wait, for even now I heard the crowing of the cock, and the dawn cannot be far off."

Then the Court broke up, and many of the younger members met together and discussed the case. And I was somewhat surprised to find that very few words of compassion were raised for Jesus. The

stubborn conduct of the prisoner had set
them against him in the first place, and
his wild outburst had confirmed their ill
thoughts of him. But most of all they
were influenced by the thought that this
was but a preliminary trial, and could only
result in handing him over to the Roman
Procurator, with whom the last word
would be. None of them had seen aught
of Jesus but during the last few days in
the Temple, when he had interfered with
their order and prerogatives. I cannot
say I was convinced, either by Hanan's
harangue at first, or by these men's ar-
guments afterwards. But I was somewhat
perplexed, feeling myself in some wise an
intruder in their midst, not being of the
priestly order. And as is my custom in
such cases, I went out into the open air
down the steps into the atrium.

There I found a great fire had been lit in
the court, for the night was chilly. Near
the fire Jesus was seated, with the High
Priest's guard around him. As I came
near, behold, one of the guard threw part
of his mantle across the face of Jesus so as
to blindfold him, and then struck him, say-

ing, " Thou art a Prophet ; prophesy who hath struck thee." And all the soldiers laughed and jeered. Then sought I the captain of the guard and told him this, and he said, " They mean naught of ill — they be rude fellows ; howbeit, I will stop them." And he went up to them and reproved them. And I paced up and down the courtyard, with the silent stars above and the glowing fire beneath, till an apparitor of the High Priest summoned me, saying, " It beginneth to dawn at the back of the house ; the Council will resume its sitting."

When I entered the council-chamber, I found all seated as before, but in the midst was a smaller table, at which was seated a scribe, with a roll in front of him. Then Hanan the High Priest came in, and said, " Ye have all had the time of deliberation prescribed by our sages in capital cases, or at least as much time as the urgency of the matter permits. We must proceed to the formal ratification of this man's sentence, for I cannot doubt that ye will see fit to confirm the righteous judgment which your zeal for the Lord caused you to pass just now upon this man. And again I would

bid you remember you are voting, not so
much for this man's death, as whether he
is to be delivered to the Romans. Scribe,
read the roll." And with that the scribe
began to read our names, and we all answered to them. Then said Hanan, "We
will now proceed to the voting," and called
upon Chananyah ben Nedebai to record
his vote. And he voted as before, for
death. Then each in his turn, and all
voted as before. And when my name was
called upon I arose and hesitated, and
Hanan looked over to me and said, "Thou
speakest here by our courtesy, Meshullam
ben Zadok; if thou disagree with the
unanimous opinion of thy colleagues, thou
hadst best instruct us in thy reasons.
What sayest thou? Is not he guilty of
death who is guilty of blasphemy against
the Most High?" "Yea," said I. "And
was not this man Jesus manifestly guilty of
blasphemy before us?" "Yea," said I.
Then said Hanan swiftly to the scribe,
"He voteth for death," and waved me
down to my seat. And thereafter all the
remaining members of the Council voted
for death, finishing with Hanan as the

oldest, who merely gave a grim nod to the scribe.

By this time it was quite light, and all the Council and many of Hanan's household joined together to say the morning prayers. After prayers most of the Council, with Hanan and Caiaphas at our head, followed the soldiers who guarded Jesus down from the Mount of Olives. As we came near the Brook Kidron, behold, a man with haggard face darted out from the shrubs by the wayside, and rushing up to Hanan the High Priest, dashed down at his feet a bag which chinked, and then disappeared into the wayside again. But Hanan only motioned with his finger to the bag at his feet, and the captain of his guard lifted it up and poured out its contents into his hand, and, behold, it was a number of new shekels from the Temple treasury. Then Hanan smiled grimly, and bade the captain put them aside. Thereupon we resumed our march, and soon came to the Aldgate. There we inquired where the Procurator was, and learnt that he had taken up his dwelling at the Palace of Herod, so that he might be in Jerusalem

during the Passover, as was his wont, for
fear of a rising at that time. Then we
marched across and halted in front of the
palace. And on our way the rumor spread
throughout the city that Jesus the Nazarene was being carried before the Procurator, and soon our procession was joined by
all who were free from household duties.
I have explained to thee, have I not, how
that for those of the older opinion this sixth
day of the week was the day on which the
Paschal lamb was to be sacrificed, and for
all good Jews the morning would be devoted to the final search after the leaven.
That morning, therefore, all the householders of Jerusalem and all the heads of
families were occupied in the search after
leaven, or in preparation for the Paschal
sacrifice, and it was only the younger men,
and those who cared not for acts of piety,
who followed our procession on the way to
Herod's Palace.

Now, all those of the Council were of
the older opinion as to the Paschal sacrifice, and were about to perform it on the
evening of that day. Wherefore it be-
hoved them not to enter the dwellings of

the heathen during that day, since it is
their custom to bury the bodies of men in
their gardens or in their houses, which
render them a defilement to us Jews.
Therefore on the day of a sacrifice no Jew
may enter a heathen's house, above all the
High Priest, upon whose sanctity the holi-
ness of the nation depends. When, therefore, we came within twenty paces of the
Procurator's dwelling, Hanan caused our
procession to halt, and a summons to be
sounded upon the trumpet. Thereat a
lictor appeared, who asked our business,
and to him Hanan gave a message to the
Procurator. And here for the first time
since he had been arrested I could see the
countenance of Jesus near me, and it surprised me much to observe that all traces
of anxiety and weariness had disappeared
from it. He seemed relieved and resigned,
and paid no heed to what was passing
around him, seeming only to commune
with himself, or perhaps, I should say, with
some inward friend and comforter.

Then Pontius Pilate came forward and
spake to Joseph Caiaphas the High Priest,
and asked him what he would with him.

And Caiaphas answered and said, pointing to Jesus, " This man have we captured and brought unto thee, finding that he was perverting the people, and declaring that he was the Anointed One of Israel, and therefore the rightful King of the Jews. Him therefore have we brought to thee, seeing it is a matter which toucheth our master the Emperor." Thereupon Pontius Pilate turned round, and said something in the barbarian tongue, and the guard of Roman soldiers came forward and took Jesus from the High Priest's guard, and took him with them up the steps of the palace. Then Pilate courteously invited the High Priests to enter the judgment-hall with him ; but they, in answer, pointed out that on that holy day they dared not enter to any house but their own and the house of God. Then Pilate turned his back with scanter courtesy, and reëntered the palace, and we and the common people remained outside waiting.

XVI.

CONDEMNATION AND EXECUTION.

XVI.

AND after a while of waiting, Pontius Pilate reappeared, and coming down to Caiaphas said, "He hath confessed; he shall join the other criminals that are to be executed this day." Then one among those who were waiting in the crowd came forward unto Pilate, and said unto him, "Master, it is a grace of our lord the Emperor that at our Passover there be released unto us one of the prisoners that are condemned to death." And Pilate answered and said, "That is so: whom will ye that I release?" And many of those in the crowd called out, "Jesus." And Pilate stepped back, and summoned to him a lictor. And shortly after soldiers came forward in the portico, bearing with them Jesus the Nazarene. Upon him was a purple robe of royalty, and upon his brow had been placed the faded rose-wreath of some reveller which had been put on in haste, and some of the thorns had torn the flesh, and blood was trickling down. When the people saw him, many cried out, " Not this Jesus, but Jesus Bar Abbas." And one man among the crowd called out, " Better Jesus Bar Abba [1] than Jesus Bar Amma; " [2] and laughter and jeers followed. Then Pilate seemed puzzled, and called to him one of his lictors, who spake earnestly to him for a time, and then received an order from him. And going up the steps, he entered the palace. And shortly afterwards there came forward the man Jesus Bar Abbas of Jerusalem, of whom I have spoken to thee before. Now, he had been very popular among the folk, and had lost his liberty in a rising against the Romans, in which a Roman sentry had been slain. And there stood the two Jesuses — the one that had risen against the Romans, and the one that had told the people they should pay tribute to their Roman lords. It was manifest that the new-comer, who had done naught against the Romans, was more in favor with Pilate the Procurator,

[1] *Bar Abba* means " son of his father."
[2] *Bar Amma* means " son of his mother." — ED.

while the folk who had welcomed him on
the first day of the week, on this the sixth
day reviled and despised him because he
had refused to lead a rising against the
Romans as the other one had done. Then
Pilate called out to them and said, "Whom
will ye that I release unto you : Jesus
who is called Bar Abbas, or Jesus who is
called Christ ? " And almost all the multitude cried, "Jesus Bar Abbas! Jesus
Bar Abbas !" Then Pilate gave command,
and the soldiers took back Jesus the Nazarene into the palace again, while others
removed the fetters from Jesus Bar Abbas,
and he came down the steps and disappeared among the crowd.

After a while, there came forward from
the side gate a company of Roman soldiers, who took their stand in front of the
steps of the palace, moving the crowd
away therefrom. And shortly after, other
soldiers brought down from above three
men, each carrying two pieces of timber,
one fixed across the top of the other, like
unto the letter *tau*. One of these was
Jesus the Nazarene, clad once more in
his own garments, and without the rose-

wreath ; yet couldst thou see the mark
of the thorns upon his brow. The others
were, as I learnt, malefactors that had
been condemned for robbery.

Just at this moment one touched me on
the shoulder, and, turning, I found it was
one of the servants of my household, who
spake unto me and said, " Meshullam ben
Zadok, thy father would speak with thee."
And as the house was not far off, I went
with him and spake to my father, who
would have me accompany him on the
search for leaven on that morn. For at
that time I was betrothed, and next year
I should have a house of my own, and
would have to conduct the search for
leaven as a master of a household. So I
went round the house with my father —
peace be upon him ! — and searched for
the leaven.

By the time the search for the leaven
had been concluded, the hour had come
for the mid-day meal, at which all the
members of my family assembled. But I
hurried forth, as soon as the grace after
meals had been said, to ascertain what
had been the fate of the Nazarene. I

could not go to the place of execution, for
it is not seemly for a member of the Sanhedrim to attend an execution. I soon
learnt that the Roman soldiers had con-
ducted Jesus and the two others to the
Hill Golgotha, somewhat apart from the
place of stoning, where our Jewish execu-
tions were held.

As I have explained to thee, Aglaophonos, our Sages have mercifully interpreted the words of the Law relating to
the four modes of capital punishment
among us — stoning, burning, beheading,
and strangulation. For stoning they have
substituted throwing down from a height
after the criminal has been made to feel
naught by drinking a mixture of frank-
incense, myrrh, and vinegar, which the
ladies of Jerusalem supply as one of their
pious duties. The criminal condemned
to be burnt is in reality strangled, and
then a lighted wick placed for a moment
in his open mouth. In every way the
aim of the Sages is to shorten the suffer-
ings of the condemned man. But the
Romans, at least in their execution of all
but Roman citizens, seem rather to aim at

the opposite of this; for they have selected, as their method of execution for
slaves and criminals that are not citizens,
suspension on a cross, by which all the
organs of the body are strained and tor-
tured till some vital organ gives way.
It was this cruel form of punishment that
the Romans were dealing out to Jesus the
Nazarene. It happeneth oft that men live
for two or three days on the cross, till
they die even of hunger. I learnt to my
dismay that Jesus had refused, with words
of menace, to take the draught of myrrh
and wine which the ladies of Jerusalem,
as I have said, prepare for all men condemned to capital punishment, so that
they may not feel the pain and torture.

I could not go to the place of execution,
as a member of the Sanhedrim. I hurried,
therefore, to the northern slopes of the
Temple mount, whence one can see Golgotha. At first I could discern naught,
for sombre clouds covered all the heights
of Scopus. But suddenly a flash came
forth from them, followed by a dull roll of
thunder, and I could see for a moment
three crosses raised side by side on the

top of Golgotha. Which of these held
Jesus I knew not. I only knew that there
was dying one who had seemed born to
do honor to his nation, to help to deliver
Israel from the men who were now tortur-
ing him to his death. Since the night before, events had so hurried past me that I
had had no time to think of their import till
now, when I sat me down in the purple
shadow of Antonia, and gazed upon the
hill of execution, where from time to time
flashes showed me the three crosses on
the hill.

This, then, was the end of the hopes
connected with Jesus of Nazara, and of
the empire which he had wielded over
men's minds! But five days agone welcomed as a king, to-day executed with the
ignominy reserved for the basest slave.
Each day of his sojourn in Jerusalem he
had made another and yet another class of
the nation his enemies. First he threatens
the power of the priests; next he insults
their opposites, the Pharisees; and then he
puts to naught the hope of the common
folk that he would help them rise against
the Romans. Between Sabbath and Sab-

bath he had lost every friend; not even
his immediate followers stood by his side
in the hour of trial.

And yet no man had appeared in Israel
for many generations endowed in so high
a degree with all the qualities which mark
us Israelites out from the nations around.
He was tender to the poor; and which of
the nations has given thought for its poor,
their feelings as well as their welfare, like
unto Israel? He bare the yoke of the
Law willingly, yet as a son, not as a slave,
of the Most High. God was to him, as
to all of us, as an ever-present Father, to
love, to chasten, and to reward; not as a
harsh taskmaster or as a boon-companion,
as with the commoner minds of thy people, Aglaophonos; nor as a vain figment
of the reason, as with thy higher minds.

Even in what thou regardest as defects
in our nation, this Jesus seemed also to
share. Thou makest us the reproach that
we give no thought to the beauties and
grandeur of nature, and in nothing that I
had seen and heard of him did the Nazarene differ from the rest of us in this.
Thou complainest that we look upon life

with all too much seriousness. " Ye cannot see the smile upon the face of things," thou saidst once to me. In this surely Jesus was a Jew of the Jews. We never saw him smile, still less heard him laugh. Thou wouldst hold up to me as a model Socrates thy teacher, who taught the Hellenes truth with a smile. That man there, dying upon the cross, had tried to teach Israel the truth with tears and threats.

Herein he followed the exemplar of our prophets. Only in Israel have the men who have led us farthest reviled us most. As our God, who has been to us a Father, has chastened us while he loved us, so our prophets have rebuked us their brethren. Many generations of men have passed since the last of the prophets spake his words of loving reproof. Now has appeared this Jesus, who again takes up their work.

But in one thing, and that a great thing, he differs from our prophets. All these spake never but as messengers of the Most High. This man alone of the prophets speaketh in his own name: therefore he hath been a stumbling-block and an of-

fence unto us.   He spake as one having
authority, and it seemed to us as arrogance.   And when we would speak with
him in the gates, and know his own
thought, he evaded our questionings and
eluded our testings.   He seemed aloof
from us and our desires.   All Israel was
pining to be freed from the Roman yoke,
and he would have us pay tribute to Rome
for aye.   Did he feel himself in some way
as not of our nation?   I know not; but
in all ways we failed to know him.

And as I was communing thus, the sun
shone forth from a rift in the clouds and
illumined for a space the crown of Calvary,
and I stretched forth my hands to the fig-
ures on the cross, and cried aloud in my
perplexity, "Jesus, what art thou?"   And
then I bethought me, and my hands fell
to my side, and I said, "What wert thou,
Jesus?"   Naught answered me but the
distant rumbling from the gloomy clouds.

But the sun was setting over Israel, and
I turned to my father's house, there once
more to celebrate the Feast of the Deliverance from Egypt.

EPILOGUE.

Thus far had I written to thee, Aglaophonos, as to what I knew of that Jesus
the Nazarene about whom thou hast made
so earnest inquiry. I had minded to hand
it to Alphæus ben Simon, my cousin, who
goeth this week in the galley to Cyprus,
and thence would have passed it on to
thee by the hands of one of our brethren
who visit Greece from year to year. But
there has happened to me an event which
has given me much to think of with regard
to this very matter of Jesus. It chanced
that the day before yesterday I went from
the Jewish quarter in this city of Alexandria for my usual walk along the Lochias,
which adjoins it. There it is my custom
to catch the sea air and to watch the ves-
sels put into the Inner Port. Now. it
chanced that as I came upon the Lochias,
the vessel of Joppa had just hoved-to in
the Inner Port, and the passengers were
being landed up the Broad Steps. Now

these, by their *talith* and their faces, I knew to be Jews, and I went up to them, and greeted them with the greeting of peace. But among them one came to me with the look of recognition in his eyes, and said, " Knowest thou me not, Meshullam ben Zadok?" And, behold, it was Rufus ben Simon, whom I had known before I left the Holy City. So I welcomed him, and brought him home to this house of mine. And here he remaineth till the morrow, when he starteth forth to go to Cyrene.

Now, in my inquiries about old friends left behind, and new things that had happened since I went away, I failed not to ask about the followers of the Nazarene. To my wonder, I found that this Rufus had become one of them, even though he was but a child when Jesus died. Yet is he a good Jew in all else. He eateth only our meat, and keepeth our Sabbaths and festivals. But he avers that the Anointed One, whom we expect, has already appeared, and that he was Jesus the Nazarene. And upon my inquiry how he could know aught of Jesus but from the common talk, he put in my hand some Memorabilia of him, written down in Hebrew by one of his chief followers, Matathias.[1] This have I read again and again, and pondered much thereon. Nor have I been able to sleep these two nights for the new thoughts about Jesus that have come to me from reading these memoirs of him.

For, behold, he appeareth in these records of him by his own followers in far other wise than he showed himself to us in public at Jerusalem. In all his public acts among us he was full of scornful rebukes; among his own followers he was tender and loving. Scarcely ever could we get him to speak out to us plainly his views about matters of public concern. He would always give us an answer full of evasion and enigma, but to his followers he would explain all his meaning over and over again, illustrated with parable. There at Jerusalem he almost always turned to the people his harsher side. I saw him on every occasion on which he appeared in

[1] Probably the so-called Primitive Gospel, the common foundation of our Synoptics. But the date is somewhat early. — ED.

public in Jerusalem, and, save only in his
sermons, he was always rebuking one or
another, just like the prophets of old. And
the manner of his rebuking towards us was
as with scorpions, whereas among his own
he would mingle tenderness even with his
reproaches.   Nor, saving his sermons,
which few heard but those who already
followed him, had he aught novel to tell us
about the things of life.   He seemed to us
as if he would destroy the temple of our
faith, nor in his public actions did he give
any promise of building it up anew.   Yet
to those with him he would continually be
telling what to do and how to do it, till,
behold, a new manner of life, fair and
seemly, stood before them, fulfilled of Jewish righteousness, with a tender mercy
which was the man's very own.

I need not detail to thee, Aglaophonos,
what these acts and words were which have
given me an altogether new light as to the
character and thoughts of the man Jesus.
From certain words of thine in thy letter,
which I understood not then when I first
read it, I can see now that thou must have
had some such account of the life and

death of Jesus before thee as this which
Rufus hath shown unto me. Now I can
understand wherefore thou hast inquired
about this Jesus with such eager insistence.
And to thee as a Gentile the revelation of
his character would come with more attractive force than to us that be Jews. For in
almost every way this Jesus fulfilleth the
idea of a Jew as we have it in these later
days. Working with his hands, yet teaching with his voice; obedient to the Law,
yet ever eager to take a new law upon himself; doing acts of love among men, yet
rebuking in love their ill acts, and doing
all things as in the presence of the Glory;
—in all this Jesus was as the best of our
Sages.

" Wherefore, then, did ye suffer him to
be killed ? " thou wilt ask me, and indeed
I ask myself. If I were to answer thee
in the way Jesus was wont to answer us,
I would say, " Why did ye Hellenes condemn Socrates to the hemlock ? " For he
was as much the Ideal of the Hellenes as
Jesus of the Jews. Every Hellene would
be eloquent and reasonable, and that was
Socrates. Every Jew would be wise and

good and pious, and that was Jesus. Yet each of these men, if I read their lives aright, died the death of a criminal, because he cared not for that which his fellow-countrymen cared for most. Socrates died because he would force his countrymen to examine by their reason the ideas and ideals which they all accepted. Jesus died for the same reason, but also for another — for that he cared naught for our national hopes. We were all panting for national freedom; he would have naught of it. Whether it was that he felt in some sort to be not of our nation, I know not; but in all his teaching he dealt with us as men, not as Jews. It is this, I can see, that has attracted thee to his doctrine, whereas thou wert always scornful of our Jewish pretensions, as thou calledst them.

Yet herein again was he at one with the best thoughts of our Sages. Our God is the God of all, and his Law shall be one day the Law of all. If we yearn for the universal realm of the Messiah, it is as much for the sake of the world as for ourselves. But methinks I see in the thoughts of this Jesus an idea quite other than ours

as to what the Anointed One shall be
and shall do. We hope for him as a Deliverer and a Conqueror with force of arms
by God's aid. Now, Jesus seemed not to
think of the Anointed One in any way
like this. His mind seemed to be filled
rather with the picture of the Servant of
God as drawn by the Prophet Esaias.
Thou knowest the passage, Aglaophonos;
I remember thy laughter when first I read
it thee, that men could look forward to
contempt and hatred as a good. Truly the
idea is far different from the saying of the
barbarian, "Woe to the conquered!" And
surely to us all, Jew and Gentile, Greek and
barbarian, the greatest of joys is this — to
worst an equal foe in fair fight. But to
Esaias the prophet, and to Jesus the Nazarene after him, the higher victory is with
him that is worsted in the battle of life.
That will come as good tidings to nine out
of every ten of men.

Therefore, if Jesus thought of himself as
the Anointed One, it was as being anointed
with the woes of the vanquished, with the
sweat and the blood of the lowly and despised. Now I know why he seemed so

sad when he was greeted at Jerusalem as a victor. He had spent his life in trying to impress a new ideal upon his people, and they had welcomed him only as the fulfilment of the old ideal which he desired to replace. None of thy poets have given a drama with more of *eironeia* in it than this.

Yet why did he remain silent before us as to these ideas of his? If, indeed, these were his ideas; for even with the new light given by the Hebrew Memorabilia, I can see his thought but dimly. Why spake he not his own thought to the people in Jerusalem, and tell us no longer to hope for worldly dominion as the best means for spreading the Law of the Lord, but rather to be as servants of God, even as Esaias the Prophet hath spoken? Was it that he wished to carry out the description of the prophet even to every iota of his text? For, behold, the prophet sayeth, "He let himself be humbled, and opened not his mouth." If so, then was the death of Jesus but a sublime suicide.

For surely by this silence he has committed a grievous sin against us his people.

For if we committed aught of sin and crime that handed him over to the Romans as a pretender to empire, he indeed shared our sin and crime by his silence. Ye Hellenes were at least greater in fault than we in the matter of Socrates; for ye condemned him after he had spoken his whole mind and made known his whole thought to his people; whereas we condemned one who, I make bold to say, was even greater than thy Socrates, mainly because of what seemed to us his sullen and arrogant silence, broken only by a confession of guilt when he knew he was not guilty.

But yet, let me not be as harsh in judgment upon him after his death, as perhaps I was when I allowed the sentence to be declared against him without protest. He, least of all men, could have died with a lie upon his lips. In some sort and in some way he must have combined the thought of the triumphant Messiah and of the despised Servant of God. For in those Memorabilia of him which have come into my hands during the last days as being a message from him that is dead, I find

these two things combined. He speaketh
ever of the blessedness of the poor and
the humble and the despised, even as
the Ebionim speak. So that if a man
would be blessed, he would choose a
lowly career, even as did Jesus. Yet
withal he speaketh oft of himself as the
Son of Man, and every Jew that heard
him would think he knew what he thereby
claimed. For in the Prophets Daniel and
Enoch it is clearly said that the Son of
Man would come in victory over the
world ; and what other could this universal
victor be than the Anointed One whom
the prophets had foretold? If Jesus put
another meaning upon the prophetic
words, why spake he not his meaning
fully unto the people? All we may have
gone like sheep astray, but he that might
have been our shepherd went apart alone
with God.

O Jesus, why didst thou not show thyself to thy people in thy true character?
Why didst thou seem to care not for aught
that we at Jerusalem cared for? Why,
arraigned before the appointed judges of
thy people, didst thou keep silence before

us, and, by thus keeping silent, share in pronouncing judgment upon thyself? We have slain thee as the Hellenes have slain Socrates their greatest, and our punishment will be as theirs. Then will Israel be even as thou wert, despised and rejected of men — a nation of sorrows among the nations. But Israel is greater than any of his sons, and the day will come when he will know thee as his greatest. And in that day he will say unto thee, " My sons have slain thee, O my son, and thou hast shared our guilt."

AFTERWORDS

TO A SECOND EDITION

It was my object in the preceding pages to present a picture of Jesus " as others saw him " at Jerusalem, so as to explain the chief *historic* problem of his career, namely, why, having entered Jerusalem on Palm Sunday amid the acclamations of the populace of Jerusalem, he was executed by the Romans five days later amid their execrations. In his utterances at Jerusalem, Jesus by no means presents that mild and persuasive figure which we associate with his name from the presentations in the Gospels of his relations to his immediate disciples. On the contrary, during Holy Week he successively alienated every section of the Jewish nation. On Monday he attacked the power of the priests, on Tuesday that of the Pharisees, while on Wednesday he set the common people against him by refusing to countenance their hopes of freedom from the Romans by acquiescing in the payment of tribute to them.

The preceding pages, therefore, may be regarded as a sort of Apologia of the Jewish people for their so-called " rejection " of Jesus. As a matter of fact, he mainly expressed movements which were already in existence among the Jewish people, as I have also endeavored to show in my description of him, and was chiefly opposed in principle to the sacerdotal party, who therefore, as a natural consequence, brought about his death after a hurried and, from a Jewish standpoint, illegal trial. By displaying the essential Jewishness of most of Jesus' doctrines I was hoping to attract the interest of Jews themselves towards the most influential figure that has appeared among them. Owing to the legends and metaphysical conceptions that have gathered round him, and the crimes that have been committed in his name, many Jews even to this day refuse to consider Jesus as a member of their race.

Another object I had in view in present-

ing a somewhat different aspect of Jesus'
life was to introduce the general reader
to the many remarkable additions to our
knowledge of his times, and even of his
own sayings, which have accumulated during the past few years.   The study of the
Talmud has contributed much new light,
and has given local color to the scenes in
which Jesus moved, while a more careful
investigation of the Apocryphal Gospels
and the Early Church Fathers has resulted
in unearthing a number of traditions and
traditional sayings of Jesus which in the
judgment of competent theologians have
nearly as much probability as those contained in the Gospels.   These extra-ca-
nonical sayings of Jesus have been collected together by Dr. Alfred Resch, under
the title of Agrapha, as the fourth part of
the fifth volume of Gebhardt and Harnack's " Texte und Untersuchungen "
(Leipsic, 1889).   I have endeavored to include the most memorable of these in the
two sermons in chapters iii. and vii.   Resch
divides his materials into Logia and Apocrypha, but there seems to me very little
difference in the amount of evidence, in

favor of the distinction, and I have used both indiscriminately. In the notes, however, which are now added, I give the number of Resch's Logia, adding a capital A. for the Apocrypha.

A word more as to the sources. I have adopted the ordinary view of the three visits of Jesus to Jerusalem during his ministry. This is of course based upon statements in the Johannine Gospel which most of the newer theologians regard as entirely apocryphal. I do not think it at all improbable that though the majority of the speeches placed in Jesus' mouth by the fourth evangelist are obviously concocted *ad hoc*, the writer may still have had access to some additional traditions which formed the excuse for his writing and the pegs on which to present his views, indeed in the same way as I myself have attempted to do in the present work.

NOTES

[The references to Resch are to the number of the Logion or Apocryphon (A.) respectively.]

Page 13. *Hanan's Bazaar.* There is a Talmudic tradition to this effect which seems to confirm the story of the cleansing of the Temple. See Derenbourg, *Histoire de la Palestine* (Paris, 1867), Appendix.

Page 15. *Approved money-changers.* Resch, 43.

Let none of alien birth. This inscription has actually been found of recent years.

Page 16. *A wheelwright.* Justin Martyr reports that Jesus made ploughs and yokes. (*Dial. c. Tryph.* c. lxxxviii.) Almost all the Jewish teachers of the time were workmen.

Page 19. *Annas.* There is no doubt that he was the most influential among the priestly party at the time that others nominally held the High Priesthood.

Page 25. *Mixture.* The actual expression in Jewish writings is *paste.*

Page 26. *Son of the Covenant.* There is, however no evidence of such custom, apart from the reference in the Gospel, till much later.

Page 30. *Wherein have I sinned.* Resch, A. 2.

Page 31. *Thou art my Son.* Resch, A. 4. Gospel account differs.

Fatherhood of God. This is of course a fundamental Jewish doctrine found throughout the earliest ritual. Cf. Deut. xxxii. 6; Jer. iii. 19; Mal. ii. 20; Ps. ciii. 13. Cf. *Jew. Quart. Rev.*, ii. 633 seq.

Page 34. *Why marvel ye?* Resch, 29.

Page 36. *Man, if thou knowest.* Resch, 27.

The Sabbath was made. This was a characteristic Jewish principle. See Derenbourg, *Histoire de la Palestine,* p. 144.

Page 41. *Let Rabbi Joshua.* This would have been Jesus' Jewish name : Rabbi was applied to all respectable persons, somewhat like our " Mr." The method of " calling up to the law " described here has lasted on to the present day.

Haphtara. The first and second lessons of the church are derived from the practice of the synagogue, where a portion of the Law is first read, and then the *Haphtara* or lesson from the prophets.

Cantillation. This has still been preserved by the synagogue; it is probably the source of the Gregorian Chant.

Page 42. *It hath been written.* This sermon has been composed out of the following sections of the Resch Agrapha : 61, 45, 20; A. 60; 12, 35; A. 76; 15, 47, 62, 9, 1, 13, 49, 48, 33, 47; A. 22; 34, 42, 26, 51, 63, 73, 65, 32, 31; A. 36; 46; A. 6; A. 29. The sentence *Howbeit, he who longs . . . till he perish* is derived from a Mohammedan tradition about Jesus. Two or three of these sayings, as, for instance, *Love covereth a multitude of sins,* occur in the Epistles, but are quoted in the Church Fathers as actual words of Jesus. Resch regards them as forming part of a Gospel now lost.

Page 48. *Let son and daughter inherit alike.* From the *Gospel according to the Hebrews,* edit. Nicholson, No. 34.

Page 49. *Let the wife.* Resch, 24. Quotation as a " Command of the Lord " by Paul, 1 Cor. xiv. 37.

Page 51. *Because they are poor.* It is a mistake to think that Jesus was the first among the Jews to insist upon the blessedness of the poor. The whole of the later literature of the Bible and the earlier literature of the Talmud bears the same tradition. See I. Loeb, *La Littérature des Pauvres dans le Bible* (Paris, 1893).

Page 57. *The Two Ways.* This is the original kernel of the *Testament of the XII. Apostles,* according to the reconstruction of Harnack, who, following Dr. Taylor, has recognized that this early catechism of the Christian Church was modelled upon a previous Jewish catechism. Traces of this latter are left in a Latin fragment in which the Christian interpolations do not appear. I have endeavored to bring out the significance of this fact from a Jewish point of view in the interviews with the Rich Young Man (page 71) and with the Scribe (page 81.) If Jesus adopted as the summing up of his own faith the ordinary statements of the common Jewish catechism of the time, it would be hard to contend that he regarded himself as in any way advancing beyond the Jewish standpoint. Harnack has given this reconstruction of the Jewish catechism in his pamphlet, *Die jüdischen beiden Wege.*

Page 67. The passage relating to the woman taken in adultery is now recognized to be an interpolation in the Gospel of St. John (in some of the earliest MSS. of which it does not occur) from a more primitive Gospel. As will be seen from the text, the contrast usually drawn between Jesus' attitude and the harshness of contemporary Jewish Law is unjustified, since Rabbinic Law had already modified the sternness of the Levitical Decree. Nothing can be more humane or tender than the address of the President of the Court on page 68, taken from the Talmudic treatise *Sota.*

Page 71. This version of the interview with the Rich Young Man is taken from the *Gospel according to the Hebrews,* edit. Nicholson, page 50. It seems to me to be more primitive than the ordinary Gospel account. The touch of the Young Man scratching his head in doubt, coarse as it is, brings the whole scene vividly before one's eyes.

Page 73. *Easier for an elephant.* This is the form in which the proverb was current among the Jews of the time, as we can see from the quotations of it in the Talmud.

Page 81. For the interview with the Scribe (whom I identify with the writer of the reminiscences) I have combined the two accounts in Luke x. and Mark xii., which obviously refer to the same incident. It is clear from the question *How readest thou?* that Jesus was referring to some written exposition of the current religion of the time. Yet the collocation of the *Shema* (Deut. vi. 4) with the injunction to neighborly love (Levit. xix. 18) does not of course occur in the Old Testament, but is found in the Jewish *Two Ways*, with some form of which Jesus is thus shown to have been acquainted.

Page 83. There is little doubt that M. Halévi is right in contending that the Parable of the Good Samaritan was originally a Parable of the Good Israelite. Jewish society was divided into three castes, Priests, Levites, and the ordinary Israelites, and the distinction is kept up even to the present day in the "calling up to the Law" (see page 40). There would be no point in referring to two of the castes if they were not to be contrasted with the third, the ordinary Israelite of the time. The point of the parable is against the sacerdotal classes, who were indeed Jesus' chief opponents and ultimately brought about his execution. As a confirmation of M. Halévi's views it may be pointed out that no Samaritan would have been found at that period on the road between Jerusalem and Jericho.

Page 92. This second sermon is put together from Resch, sections 23, 68; A. 57; A. 27, 53, 18, 21, 25, 7, 41; A. 11; 17, 16, 10, 5, 64, 36 b, 52, 60, 59, 39. The two passages, *Is it not enough for the disciples to be as the Master?* and *I will choose me the good whom my*

Father in the heavens hath given me, are from the *Gospel according to the Hebrews,* edit. Nicholson, Nos. 13, 14.

Page 96. *Awake thou.* Quoted by Paul, Eph. v. 14. See Resch, 37.

Page 102. This description of an ordinary Jewish meal of the time is taken from the Talmudic indications as given in S. Spitzer, *Das Mahl bei den alten Hebräern.* The blessing on the bread is that said up to the present day.

Page 103. *Fowl to be boiled in milk.* This was one of the points in dispute between the Galileans and the Jews of the time. See Talmud, *Chullin,* 116 a.

Page 105. *Corban.* This is the actual word used in the Greek original, but on the rather subtle point raised by Jesus there was a division of opinion among the Jewish doctors, as stated in the text. It is somewhat curious that only upon this and the question of washing hands before meals is there record of a specific difference between Jesus and the teaching of the Pharisees.

Page 109. *Many a Pharisee.* This is from the celebrated division of Pharisees into seven classes, made in the Talmud.

King Jannaus. From the Talmud. This shows that the dangers of hypocritical observances of the externalities of the Law were recognized a hundred years before Jesus.

Page 113. *Hall of hewn stone.* See Derenbourg, *Histoire de la Palestine.*

Page 114. I have selected these sayings from John as typifying the attitude of Jesus which would most grate against Jewish feeling. It is the seeming arrogance of these statements which forms the chief jarring note in the Gospels, judged from a Jewish point of view. How far they are authentic, however, is a very grave question. The whole tendency of modern criticism is to regard them as apocryphal.

Page 118. *O Jerusalem, Jerusalem!* Resch, 58.

Page 120. *Signs of the times.* For these, see Drummond, *Jewish Messiah.*

Page 123. *Jesus Bar Abbas.* The earliest MSS. of the Gospels give this as the full form of Barabbas' name, and it is necessary to remember this as a clue to the scene at the Prætorium. See p. 198. Though ordinarily spoken of as a robber, it is clear from Mark xv. 7 that Barabbas had been concerned in some insurrection against the Romans.

Page 125. *Maccabee.* The ordinary etymology of this word is from the Hebrew for "hammer." Cf. Charles Martel.

Page 127. *Hosanna Barabba.* Some of the Apocryphal Gospels give this in the Aramaic form.

Page 142. *Street of the Bakers.* Mentioned in Jeremiah xxxvii. 21.

Page 147. *Jochanan ben Zaccai.* If the ordinary date given for Hillel be correct, Jochanan would have been the chief Rabbi of the time of Jesus.

Page 163. *Peter, of whom.* An addition in Tatian's *Diatessaron,* recently discovered. Whether authentic or not, it clearly shows that the early Christians felt a need of explanation with regard to Jesus' seemingly unpatriotic acquiescence in paying tribute to Rome. It is at any rate clear that it was this incident that set the common people against Jesus, and enabled the sacerdotal party to compass his death.

Page 169. *Passover lamb to be killed.* I have adopted Chwolson's ingenious explanation of the discrepancy between John and the Synoptics in his treatise *Das Passahmahl Christi,* 1893.

Page 171. *Moon, which was near its full.* We know that the moon must have been full at this date, since the Hebrew months are lunar ones.

Page 172. *Priestly Sanhedrim.* Derenbourg has

made it probable that the Greater Sanhedrim, of seventy-one members, was composed of three orders of Lesser Sanhedrim, each containing twenty-three; the addition of President and Vice-President would make the number seventy-one. The three orders were those of the Jews of that time and of this, namely, Priests, Levites, and Israelites. If, as is probable, the Trial of Jesus before the Sanhedrim took place outside of Jerusalem at the house of Hanan, it is likely that he was only tried before the priestly section, who indeed would be most embittered against him.

Page 173. *Mount of Olives.* It has not been observed, I think, that if a trial took place before the Sanhedrim it must have been outside the walls of Jerusalem, since on passing through the gates of the city manned by the Roman soldiery Jesus would have had to be delivered up to the latter.

Page 174. *Many of their names.* The names which follow are those of the High Priests immediately preceding and succeeding Jesus' death. They would therefore be members of the Sanhedrim at that time.

Page 176. *Character of the man Pontius Pilate.* The anecdotes which follow are authentic, and show that Pilate was harsh and tyrannical.

Page 179. *Judas.* The Talmud reports that Jesus was condemned on the testimony of concealed witnesses, and I think it by no means unlikely that some such scene occurred. It is difficult to explain the execration with which Judas' memory was regarded by the early Church, if he had merely pointed out Jesus to the Roman soldiery.

Wise provision of our Law. The trial of Jesus was under any circumstances illegal according to Jewish Law.

Page 186. *Thou art the youngest.* This was one of the wise provisions of Jewish Law.

Page 191. *Search after leaven.* On the day preceding

the Passover, the head of a Jewish household has to perform this search after leaven. It must therefore have been a rabble that crowded round the Prætorium.

Page 193. *Dared not enter to any house.* This is a point mentioned by John alone, and seems to prove that he had some independent testimony.

Page 197. *Faded rose-wreath.* One can only explain the so-called crown of thorns in some such way as this. No one desiring to torture another would first torture himself still more, as any one would have to do to make a crown of thorns.

Page 198. *Jesus.* It is only by remembering that Barabbas' name was also Jesus that we can understand the scene before the Prætorium. See Note on page 123.

Page 201. *Four modes of capital punishment.* This proves that Jesus' death was according to Roman, not to Jewish Law, which only gave instantaneous death for capital punishment.

Page 202. *Words of menace.* Luke xxiii. 28–31. It is probable that these not over-kind words were said in response to the offer of the anæsthetic, made, according to the merciful custom of the time, by the ladies of Jerusalem.

Page 208. *Rufus ben Simon.* A real personage.

Page 209. *Appeareth in these records.* It is forgotten, when judging of the conduct of the Jews of Jerusalem, that they never saw him in any of his attractive aspects.

Page 216. *Daniel and Enoch.* The latter is quoted as scripture in the Epistle of St. Jude. For the use of the expression *Son of Man* in it, see the *Excursus* of Charles in his translation of Enoch.

THE JEWISH PEOPLE

HISTORY • RELIGION • LITERATURE

AN ARNO PRESS COLLECTION

Agus, Jacob B. **The Evolution of Jewish Thought**: From
Biblical Times to the Opening of the Modern Era. 1959

Ber of Bolechow. **The Memoirs of Ber of Bolechow**
(1723-1805). Translated from the Original Hebrew MS. with an
Introduction, Notes and a Map by M[ark] Vishnitzer. 1922

Berachya. **The Ethical Treatises of Berachya, Son of Rabbi**
Natronai Ha-Nakdan: Being the Compendium and the Masref.
Now edited for the First Time from MSS. at Parma and Munich
with an English Translation, Introduction, Notes, etc. by
Hermann Gollancz. 1902

Bloch, Joseph S. **My Reminiscences.** 1923

Bokser, Ben Zion, **Pharisaic Judaism in Transition**: R. Eliezer
the Great and Jewish Reconstruction After the War with Rome.
1935

Dalman, Gustaf. **Jesus Christ in the Talmud, Midrash, Zohar,**
and the Liturgy of the Synagogue. Together with an
Introductory Essay by Heinrich Laible. Translated and Edited
by A. W. Streane. 1893

Daube, David. **The New Testament and Rabbinic Judaism.** 1956

Davies, W. D. **Christian Origins and Judaism.** 1962

Engelman, Uriah Zevi. **The Rise of the Jew in the Western**
World: A Social and Economic History of the Jewish People
of Europe. Foreword by Niles Carpenter. 1944

Epstein, Louis M. **The Jewish Marriage Contract**: A Study
in the Status of the Woman in Jewish Law. 1927

Facets of Medieval Judaism. 1973. New Introduction by
Seymour Siegel

The Foundations of Jewish Life: Three Studies. 1973

Franck, Adolph. **The Kabbalah, or, The Religious Philosophy**
of the Hebrews. Revised and Enlarged Translation [from the
French] by Dr. I. Sossnitz. 1926

Goldman, Solomon. **The Jew and The Universe.** 1936

Gordon, A. D. **Selected Essays.** Translated by Frances Burnce
from the Hebrew Edition by N. Teradyon and A. Shohat,
with a Biographical Sketch by E. Silberschlag. 1938

Ha-Am, Achad (Asher Ginzberg). **Ten Essays on Zionism and**
Judaism. Translated from the Hebrew by Leon Simon. 1922.
New Introduction by Louis Jacobs

Halevi, Jehudah. **Selected Poems of Jehudah Halevi.**
Translated into English by Nina Salaman, Chiefly from the
Critical Text Edited by Heinrich Brody. 1924

Heine, Heinrich. **Heinrich Heine's Memoir**: From His Works,
Letters, and Conversations. Edited by Gustav Karpeles;
English Translation by Gilbert Cannan. 1910. Two volumes in one

Heine, Heinrich. **The Prose Writings of Heinrich Heine.** Edited, with an Introduction, by Havelock Ellis. 1887

Hirsch, Emil G[ustav]. **My Religion.** Compilation and Biographical Introduction by Gerson B. Levi. **Including The Crucifixion Viewed from a Jewish Standpoint:** A Lecture Delivered by Invitation Before the "Chicago Institute for Morals, Religion and Letters." 1925/1908

Hirsch, W. **Rabbinic Psychology:** Beliefs about the Soul in Rabbinic Literature of the Talmudic Period. 1947

Historical Views of Judaism: Four Selections. 1973

Ibn Gabirol, Solomon. **Selected Religious Poems of Solomon Ibn Gabirol.** Translated into English Verse by Israel Zangwill from a Critical Text Edited by Israel Davidson. 1923

Jacobs, Joseph. **Jesus as Others Saw Him:** A Retrospect A. D. 54. Preface by Israel Abrahams; Introductory Essay by Harry A. Wolfson. 1925

Judaism and Christianity: Selected Accounts, 1892-1962. 1973. New Preface and Introduction by Jacob B. Agus

Kohler, Kaufmann. **The Origins of the Synagogue and The Church.** Edited, with a Biographical Essay by H. G. Enelow. 1929

Maimonides Octocentennial Series, Numbers I-IV. 1935

Mann, Jacob. **The Responsa of the Babylonian Geonim as a Source of Jewish History.** 1917-1921

Maritain, Jacques. **A Christian Looks at the Jewish Question.** 1939

Marx, Alexander. **Essays in Jewish Biography.** 1947

Mendelssohn, Moses. **Phaedon; or, The Death of Socrates.** Translated from the German [by Charles Cullen]. 1789

Modern Jewish Thought: Selected Issues, 1889-1966. 1973. New Introduction by Louis Jacobs

Montefiore, C[laude] G. **Judaism and St. Paul:** Two Essays. 1914

Montefiore, C[laude] G. **Some Elements of the Religious Teaching of Jesus According to the Synoptic Gospels.** Being the Jowett Lectures for 1910. 1910

Radin, Max. **The Jews Amongs the Greeks and Romans.** 1915

Ruppin, Arthur. **The Jews in the Modern World.** With an Introduction by L. B. Namier. 1934

Smith, Henry Preserved. **The Bible and Islam;** or, The Influence of the Old and New Testaments on the Religion of Mohammed. Being the Ely Lectures for 1897. 1897

Stern, Nathan. **The Jewish Historico-Critical School of the Nineteenth Century.** 1901

Walker, Thomas [T.] **Jewish Views of Jesus:** An Introduction and an Appreciation. 1931. New Introduction by Seymour Siegel

Walter, H. **Moses Mendelssohn:** Critic and Philosopher. 1930

Wiener, Leo. **The History of Yiddish Literature in the Nineteenth Century.** 1899

Wise, Isaac M. **Reminiscences.** Translated from the German and Edited, with an Introduction by David Philipson. 1901